Northrop
F-89
Scorpion
A Photo Chronicle

Marty J. Isham &
David R. McLaren

Schiffer Military/Aviation History
Atglen, PA

Front cover artwork by Steve Ferguson, Colorado Springs, CO.

TIGER'S EYE
The cover depicts an F-89D of the 437th FIS "Tigers" flying out of Oxnard AFB California in the 1950's era. The interceptro team has made visual contact on their radar vector, yet another commercial airliner cruising down the California coast. The Tigers' mission in the most heavily armed interceptor of that decade fell within the North American defense network for cities and industries, which obviously never afforded them a true warriors' environment. Live firing took place at remote locations, the most notable being the annual exercise held at the Yuma, Arizona, USAF Firing Range. Inevitably, squadron rivalries there resulted in a scoring system which gave birth to an officially sanctioned competition designated as the Yuma Gunnery Meet. In 1956, the Oxnard Tigers proved their worth by winning the Yuma Gunnery Meet Rocketry Team Championship.

Dedication
To Peter E. Cootware, my uncle,
he liked airplanes, too.
He started my love affair with airplanes....Marty

Book Design by Ian Robertson.

Copyright © 1996 by Marty J. Isham & David R. McLaren.
Library of Congress Catalog Number: 96-67280

Printed in China.
ISBN: 0-7643-0065-2

We are interested in hearing from authors with book ideas on related topics.

Published by Schiffer Publishing Ltd.
77 Lower Valley Road
Atglen, PA 19310
Please write for a free catalog.
This book may be purchased from the publisher.
Please include $2.95 postage.
Try your bookstore first.

Contents

Introduction

As was the case with many historical aircraft, whom you discussed the aircraft with and what their personal opinion of the machine was, provided you with the information to determine whether or not it was a good aircraft. While technical information provides the solid facts, it carries its own antiseptic lack of objectivity. Some Scorpion crews considered the F-89 to be the Cadillac of fighters during its era, while others compared it to a sluggish truck. It was as large as a World War II medium bomber, and compared with its diminutive predecessors or its contemporaries, it was just too big to be a fighter. In fact, although it bore a fighter's designation, it was not, nor had it ever been intended to be, a fighter per se. The F-89 was designed to be an interceptor of enemy bombers, and not a dog-fighter among enemy fighters. It was a smooth and rock-stable aircraft with a roomy cockpit, but it was slow to accelerate and climb. Regardless, it was definitely an aircraft whose reputation proceeded it with some trepidation. As one ex-Air Force pilot stated, "The vacume (sic) cleaner was not a good portion of my career."

The Scorpion entered the Air Force's inventory with several shortcomings and a propensity for engine failures brought on by fledgling technology and the ingestion of foreign objects into its engines, due to the low slung intake's ability to suck up any and everything that might be laying loose on the ramps and runways. Early engine life was a bare twenty hours between major overhauls.

Soon after, word of these problems spread around the Air Force, catastrophic wing failures occurred on several F-89s, the most notable of which occured at what was then the major air show in the United States at Detroit, Michigan. This incident was captured by several alert photographers and their photographs were widely published. Coupled with the knowledge of the early failures of the aircraft's empanage, the F-89 was looked upon with a jaundiced view by most observers who thought that the Scorpion was just too big to be a fighter to begin with.

The wing and tail problems were cured by Northrop engineers, and the foreign object problem was solved by installing retractable inlet screens and educating air force personnel to keep the ramps, taxiways, and runways clean, and the F-89 became operational with crews who soon learned to cope with its few remaining shortcomings and exploit the interceptor's features.

Although the first flights of the XP-89 were conducted in the same time period as the other aircraft it was competing with for the United States Air Force contracts, accidents and incidents, along with production delivery problems delayed its being truly assigned to USAF operational squadrons until long after some of the other competitors had become operational. In fact, in practical numbers, some of the stopgap F-94As that the early F-89 had contended with for the initial USAF contracts were already slated for second-line service with the Air National Guard by the time the F-89 entered the USAF inventory in sufficient numbers, at which time the F-89 replaced these aircraft in many squadrons. Poetic justice, perhaps. Of all the USAF all-weather fighter-interceptors of the two decades encompassing the F-89's existence, from the P-61 to the F-104, it was the only one never to be placed in a combat environment somewhere around the world, nevertheless it did serve its country well in the role for which it was intended.

OPPOSITE:The Bell XP-83, an enlarged version of their ground-breaking XP-59, was originally proposed as an all-weather interceptor. -Bell Textron

Chapter One: In The Beginning

The General Operational Requirements, GORs, that eventually evolved into the F-89 Scorpion were given to aircraft manufacturers on August 28, 1945, for consideration and possible competition of prototype aircraft. These initial requirements called for a long-range, all-weather penetration and interceptor fighter—a mighty broad scope. The specifications called for a combat radius of 600 statute miles, a speed of 550 mph at sea level and 525 mph at 35,000 feet, which had to be attainable in twelve minutes. It was expected, although not mandated, that the future aircraft would be conventionally powered.

Six aircraft manufacturers responded to the GOR: Bell, Consolidated (soon to be Convair), Curtiss, Douglas, Goodyear, and Northrop were the initial contenders. But with the Post-war shutdowns affecting all aircraft production, Goodyear quickly dropped out of aircraft production entirely. Bell dropped out to concentrate on their XP-83 penetration fighter proposal under a separate GOR, and Convair to concentrate on the B-36 and their future innovative XP-92. Douglas Aircraft Corporation and chief engineer Ed Heinemann, long involved with the US Navy, remained in contention for three years with their XF3D Skyknight program, and in spite of their proposal not being accepted by the Air Force, they pursued it for the Navy and wound up with an all-weather fighter that remained in service longer than any of the others that mentioned here. This left Curtiss with their design for the XP-87 and Northrop, who had submitted four different designs. Two of these designs were similar, designated as "A" and "B," with the first powered by General Electric TG-180 engines, and the second by Westinghouse 24-Cs. Designs "C" and "D" were also similar to each other, but were tailless, with "C" having two engines, and "D" with three.

Of the later designs submitted by Jack Northrop, designer and founder of the Northrop Aircraft Corporation, they were based upon his fascination with the futuristic flying wing type of aircraft. The XP-79 was his answer to the Lockheed Aircraft Corporation XP-80 Shooting Star, but unfortunately the single prototype XP-79, 43-52437, which was revised several times and eventually would become the XP-79B, crashed on its maiden flight on September 12, 1945. At this time Northrop began concentrating on other flying wing aircraft, the future XB-35, and the later improvement of its design that evolved into the long-range XB-49, YB-49, and YRB-49A. All of these aircraft eventually lost out in a combination of a political contract contention with the B-36 and a problem that could not be overcome at the time, that of a constant wing flutter which made accurate bombing or photography impossible.

In more conventional terms, Northrop had a definite advantage in competition specified by the GOR for the all-weather fighter. Northrop had previously developed, and was still building at the time of the GOR issuance, the P-61 Black Widow night fighter and its off-shoot the F-15 Reporter, a long-range reconnaissance aircraft. The P-61 was the first Allied fighter to be dedicated from scratch to fulfill the role of an all-weather fighter. Northrop's engineers and design teams were already familiar with radar and armament systems, including the required (at the close up time of the first GOR), its ability to function as an interdiction fighter with the ability to carry and fire/drop underwing rockets and other external ordnance.

The first contract under this GOR for an all-weather fighter went to Curtiss for their XP-87 Nighthawk, which was issued on November 21, 1945. This design was based upon their original proposal for an attack aircraft that was designated as the XA-43. This particular aircraft never got beyond the design stage, and funding and the original serial number allocation was then transferred to the XP-87. Curtiss' new fighter, as with Northrop's selected design, would be jet propelled. It would be powered by four J-34 engines that produced a bare 3,000 pounds of thrust each. Inadequate under all conditions, the design was modified to become the XP-87A Blackhawk equipped two J-47 engines, but this example, although physically completed, was never flown.

Convair's XF-92A was once placed under the same GOR, that resulted in the F-89 contract. It never became an operational fighter, serving as a test bed for the delta wing configuration. Its design later evolved into the F-102. -Convair

OPPOSITE: The prototype XF-89 after modifications, which included the addition of 600 gallon tiptanks. -Northrop Grumman Corp.

Competing in the all-weather interceptor competition was the Curtiss XP-87 (top). Initially powered by four XJ-34-WE-7 engines that produced a bare 3000 pounds static thrust, it was re-engined with two J-47-GE-15s and became the XP-87A (lower). A contract for 88 examples of these was issued, but it was canceled and effectively put Curtiss out of the aviation business. -Air Force Museum via David Menard.

The YF-89A. Evident are the exhaust deflectors to control the engines efflux. Northrop spent thousands of man-hours in attempting to control the engine's exhaust, because of its detrimental effect upon the aircraft's empanage. -Northrop Grumman Corp.

The second F-89A was delivered to the USAF on October 3, 1950, under Project Air Material Command -OPF-80, never having been intended for combat usage. On September 17, 1952, it was redesignated as a EDF-89A (Exempt, Drone controller), and then later in its career it was transferred to the U. S. Army at Cocoa Beach, Florida, for their own drone programs. -Northrop Grumman Corp.

On April 10, 1946, Northrop was chosen to construct the XP-89 and on June 13 they received a Letter Contract from the Air Force's Air Material Command's Procurement Division to produce two two-place, twin-engine jet propelled prototypes under Fiscal Year 1946 funds. Initially they were given $4 million dollars for start-up costs. Further contract negotiations took place within the following year and on May 21, 1947, the contract was increased by $1.6 million dollars. The first example, designated as Northrop's model N-24, was given the Air Force serial number of 46-678, and it was to be available for testing no later than September 1948.

Under the GOR, Northrop engineers were faced with several problems, none insurmountable considering their pre-

The YF-89A, 46-679 in flight with the revised slender 300 gallon tiptanks. Note that the canopy is slightly more bulbous than those later found on production models. -Northrop Grumman Corp.

vious experience. Paramount was the installation of the radar and armament systems, the position of the proposed twin jet engines, and the general layout of the aircraft.

The most obvious solution to the first was to place the radar and specified cannons in the aircraft's nose, where the radar would have an uninterrupted scan, and the cannon's field of fire would be directly forward. The next situation was the placement of the engines and their enormous intakes, which produced extensive drag. If the engines were located within the aircraft's fuselage with the intakes protruding, the fuselage's cross-section would be effected, so the most logical placement would be directly behind the intakes. This was a procedure in contrast to the McDonnell Aircraft Corporation's XF-88 and the Lockheed Aircraft Corporation's XF-90, which had their engines buried deep into their fuselages. The placement of the XP-89s engines also made for much simpler, and far quicker, engine maintenance. This was a critical item, as engine reliability was a bare twenty hours between engine overhauls during this period.

Thus placed, wing/fuselage drag was also reduced to a minimum by the placement of the engines, which kept the leading edge of the wing "clean" from the intakes. The wing itself was conventional high aspect (the ratio of chord to span), laminar flow, which placed the aerodynamic "burble" as far to its trailing edge as possible. It was the fastest sub-sonic wing known at the time, and the airfoil was based upon the NACA 0009-64 design.

With the low placement of the engines, the location of the horizontal stabilizer did cause some initial problems, as it was affected by the engines' efflux. Originally placed low on the vertical stabilizer, just above its junction with the fuselage, the horizontal stabilizer was found to be adversely af-

F-89A 49-2433 was utilized to fulfill the obligation to demonstrate that the Scorpion could be used as a fighter-bomber, and mandated by the initial GOR. It was assigned to the 2759th TEG at Edwards AFB, California, and stuck in this unnecessary program between January 1951 and November 1952. It eventually wound up as an instructional airframe at Hill AFB, Utah. -USAF AFFTC

fected by both engine exhaust and the airflow over the aircraft's fuselage in wind tunnel tests. The solution was to move it higher on the vertical stabilizer where it would not be "blanked-out" by the wing's airflow when the aircraft was in an high angle of attack attitude, as while landing.

This did lead to another problem, which became more severe as the aircraft's development progressed. The cruciform tail design split the airflow both above and below the horizontal stabilizer. When the airflow met the vertical stabi-

lizer it split again, to the left and right of the vertical fin and rudder. This situation created both drag and adverse turbulence upon the elevators and rudder and a loss in their effectiveness. The solution here was to place the leading edge of the horizontal stabilizer ahead of the leading edge of the vertical stabilizer, so the air could split up and down before it was expanded to the left and right. DeHavilland Aircraft in Great Britain had solved a similar problem on their Vampire by installing a "bullet" at the junction of these surfaces that created an artificial airflow by breaking up the aerodynamic forces.

49-2435 was named "Working Girl" by Northrop's test pilots, and Chris Christofferson made its 200th test flight with a drag chute installed for the required spin tests. The chute separated from its retaining cable, but he recovered from the spin without further problems. -Northrop Grumman Corp.

49-2438 was the last of the actual F-89As and it spent most of its early career on bailment to the Allison Engine Division of General Motors at Indianapolis, Indiana, for engine development tests. In May 1954 it became a JF-89A and then was utilized as a support aircraft for the new F-89H program. In June 1957 it was transferred to Edwards AFB as a display aircraft. -Air Force Museum

Assigned to the Air Proving Ground at Eglin AFB, Florida, 49-2447 was the last of the F-89As built, but it was modified to F-89B-5 standards before acceptance by the USAF. -Tom Cuddy

Northrop's F-89A production line, the majority of which would be modified to B standards. The early ejection seats are noteworthy, as they had just been tested three years previously in another Northrop product, the P-61. Also noteworthy is the deflection gauge for the aileron installation accuracy. -Northrop Grumman corp.

The prototype XP-89 was to be powered by two General Electric designed TG-180 engines, which were later produced by the Allison Engine Division of General Motors and identified as J35-A-13s that became the standard axial flow powerplants of the era. They only produced 3,800 pounds of thrust and did not feature afterburners. As the future would show, the P-89 would become continually heavier and heavier, and although the engines would also be continually changed and improved, an adequate engine to balance out the aircraft's increasing weight to thrust ratio would never be found.

The Air Material Command, AMC, took their first look at the XP-89 mockup in September 1946, and they were "not favorably impressed." They were not happy with the fuselage fuel tanks being located over the engines' hot sections, as they appeared in a hazardous position under normal conditions and in the event of battle damage they would be in an extremely dangerous location. The oil systems needed reworking. The cockpit area needed modification to place the crew in closer proximity to each other, as the radar observer's position was too far aft, and the canopy design over the entire enclosure needed to be redone. Northrop had planned extensive use of magnesium in wing construction, but the Air Force wanted aluminum as it was less volatile in a fire, and also less expensive. One of the initial requirements was deleted, however, and that was the installation of a tail mounted turret armament system. In December the AMC got another look at the mock-up and suggested further changes, but they did give the go-ahead for the construction of the prototype.

On February 15, 1948, Curtiss flew their XP-87 for the first time. Because it was only able to attain 450 mph, authority was given to them to re-engine the fighter that they had proposed for the interceptor role.

On September 18, 1947, the Air Force became an independent branch of military service and became the United States Air Force, USAF. On January 13, 1948, all "Army Air Fields" were changed to Air Bases or Air Force Bases, depending upon their location. On June 11, 1948, all "P" for Pursuit designations were changed to "F" for Fighter, something more akin to the aircraft's roles. The XP-89 thus became the XF-89 at this time.

Taxi tests of the prototype XF-89 commenced on August 12, 1948, and on August 16, Northrop test pilot Fred Bretcher flew the XF-89 for the first time, some six months later than originally anticipated. Conducted from Muroc Air Force Base, CA, Bretcher detected a fuel siphon problem and aborted the flight after only eleven minutes. Other than complaining of a lack of rudder control force, there were no other aerodynamic complaints or problems. (Muroc was a reversal of the name of the area's original land owner's name, Corum. In Decem-

Built specifically for testing under Project APG-1PF-288, 49-2450 became a F-89B-10 and was assigned to the 3203rd Test & Evaluations Group at Eglin AFB. The crewman is working inside of one of the many "Hell Holes" in the F-89, the battery compartment, where the heat could become stifling. -Esposito

51-5850 was from the last block of F-89Cs, a C-40, The C model weighed 24, 512 pounds empty, or grossed 37, 619 when fully loaded. -Esposito

ber 1949 it was renamed as Edwards Air Force Base after a test pilot who was killed flying one of Northrop's B-49s).

Meeting on September 7-8, 1948, a USAF board recommend that the USAF procure the F-89 over the Curtiss XF-87A and the aforementioned F3D Skynight that Douglas had placed in contention, which was first flown in March 1948 and was well along in development. Also proposed by Lockheed at this time was a modification of their XP-90 long-range penetration fighter as an all-weather fighter. In making their selection, the USAF conceded that the XF-89 was "the best of a poor lot" to select from.

Due to foreseen problems with the XF-89 the USAF "hedged their bet" by issuing a new GOR for another all-weather interceptor. This new GOR led to contracts for the North American Aviation Corporation for modification of their F-86A by adding an afterburner and radar equipment and the resultant fighter was designated the XF-95, which was later redesignated as the F-86D. Lockheed submitted their own proposal for a modification of their new TF-80C two-seat jet trainer to similar specifications, adding an afterburner and

radar, and converting the second cockpit to a radar operator's position. This effort resulted in the F-94.

Northrop pilots made the next seven XF-89 flights, and flights nine through twelve were made in mid-September by pilots from Wright-Patterson AFB, home of the Air Material Command.

On October 14, 1948, General Muir Fairchild ordered the F-89 into production as soon as possible. This declaration was reinforced on November 10 when Secretary of Defense James Forrestal concurred. Forrestal also signed a contract with Lockheed for two prototype YF-94s, along with placing an order for 150 examples, to be built with Fiscal Year 1949 funds. (This number would be reduced to 110 F-94As). At this same time the contract with Curtiss for eighty F-87s was canceled; in favor of the funding for the Northrop contract. Curtiss, the original producer of aircraft for the US military, was now effectively out of the aircraft production business, as they had no other designs forthcoming.

On January 10, 1949, President Harry Truman released the funds for the procurement of forty-eight F-89s and the 110 F-94As. Northrop would receive $51 million for this project, including $3 million Cost-Plus-A-Fixed-Fee for their expenditures. The contract called for the modification of the second XF-89, 46-679, to YF-89 standards. The usual practice of designating the first example as "X" and the following thirteen as "Y" (for service tests), had been dropped.

On January 13, the USAF announced their Advanced Development Objective, ADO, for the "1954 Interceptor," the year it was expected to become operational. This ADO integrated the aircraft's weapons system with the proposed aircraft for the first time, in contrast with designing the aircraft independently, and then adding the armament. Designated as Project MX-1554, the competitors were Republic, North American, Lockheed, Chance Vought, Douglas, and Convair. The initial winners were Convair with their XF-102 improvement of their previous XF-92 effort, Republic with the XF-103, and North American Aviation with the XF-107. North American soon changed their mind and decided that the XF-107 was more suited for the fighter-bomber role, and dropped from contention in this interceptor program.

This second Scorpion would soon be redesignated, after desired modifications, to become the first XF-89A. The contract also called for one static test airframe, sans engines, avionics, and other internal equipment, for physical testing to destruction: to determine just how robust the airframe was. Also to be included were spare parts, ground handling equipment, and other ancillary equipment.

Also in January 1949, the USAF again hedged their bet on the F-89 program by authorizing North American Aviation to continue with the development with the XF-95, considering it a "gap-filler" between the F-89 and the future F-102. (This F-102 program was called the "1954 Interceptor" which had its roots stemming from Convair's XF-92. The XF-92 had made its maiden flight on September 18, 1948.) North American Aviation started preliminary design work on the XF-95 in

NORTHROP F-89D SCORPION

Appearing to be not much more than rows of pointed sticks, the 104 2.75" HVARs of the new F-89Ds armament. -McLaren Collection

March, and the construction of two prototypes commenced in May. On July 19, three weeks after the crash landing of the XF-89 at Muroc, Secretary of the Air Force Stuart Symington approved the expenditures of $7 million dollars to further the Sabre program.

Phase I flight testing of the XF-89 began in February 1949 and continued routinely until June 14, when it was completed after a total of forty-eight flights. At this time Phase II commenced. Then, on June 27, the prototype was damaged in a forced landing at Muroc. During this incident it was flown by USAF pilot Lt. Colonel C. C. Moon, with civilian R. V. Coleman acting as an observer. The cause of the incident was due to the pressurization of the landing gear wheel wells, which was brought on by a misalignment of the landing gear doors and ambient air pressure during a high speed low pass that forced a wheel into the airstream, which resulted in the loss of the left landing gear. Repaired, the interceptor was demonstrated to USAF personnel in July, by which time it was already a year behind schedule. At this time, the competing YF-94 was also already undergoing flight tests, having been flown for the first time on April 16. (In a bit of an historical oddity, the YF-94 was still designated as a YTF-80C at this time and would not officially be identified as a YF-94 until April 1950).

On May 13, while initial F-89 flight testing was under way, the USAF issued Northrop contract AF33(038)-1817 for forty-eight F-89As, serial numbered for Fiscal Year 1949, 49-2431/-2478. The initial order involved $39 million. In spite of all the problems and delays, in October 1949 the USAF authorized the construction of an additional sixty-four F-89As, for a total of 112 examples. Also in October, after having just made its first flight in September, the USAF authorized the construction of 122 additional F-86Ds. At this time the ADC selected the F-86D as their defensive weapon of choice over the F-89 and F-94 until the F-102 could be developed. Two thousand, five hundred and four of these "gap filler" F-86Ds were built, 500 more than the combined production of F-89s and F-94s.

Northrop's second example, the YF-89, 46-679, finally took to the air on November 15, 1949. This aircraft was offi-cially accepted by the USAF in January 1950, while Northrop continued to "own" the first example.

The prototype XF-89 was lost on its 102nd flight near Hawthorne, California, on February 22, 1950, with disastrous results, crashing in front of a gathering of AMC officials. Northrop pilot Charles Tucker and flight engineer Arthur Turton were making a high-speed low pass for the observers when the skin on the right horizontal stabilizer peeled off, and then the entire empennage separated from the XF-89. As the aircraft disintegrated Tucker was thrown clear and parachuted down, while Turton was killed in the crash. The cause for this accident was found to be a high-frequency low-amplitude flutter of both the vertical and horizontal stabilizers that was induced by the engine's exhaust pattern. This accident forced a curtailment of production of the Scorpion program while efforts to improve the YF-89 took place.

Several major changes were made on the aircraft at this time, including the substitution of the J-35A-17 engines to J-35A-17As fitted with afterburners, as the prototype had definitely been underpowered and suffered from a lack of acceleration, a poor rate of climb and an inability to come even close to its proposed service ceiling, and an insufficient range. Later the YF-89 would receive J-35A-21 engines, which produced 4,900 pounds thrust and offered a slight improvement in all facets.

Another major modification was to increase the aircraft's nose length by three feet, for a total of fifty-three feet. Now designated as the YF-89A, the modified YF-89A was first flown as such on June 27, 1950. Northrop believed that the aircraft, now officially named the "Scorpion," was as good as "the state of the art at the moment would permit."

Even though the future F-89A had been held up, the USAF accepted the first example (49-2431) of the contracted production series for them on September 28, 1950, after Northrop pilot John J. Quinn flew it from Mines Field (Los Angeles International Airport) to Edwards AFB on September 25. Quinn, a MIT graduate, had come to Northrop from Lockheed after working on the competitor F-94 project as a flight test engineer. The USAF also accepted the second example, 49-2432, on October 3, and the third example, 49-2435, on December 11. By this time the competing F-94A was already in operational service, having been assigned to the 325th and 52nd Fighter Interceptor Groups in the Spring of 1950 and the 449th Fighter Interceptor Squadron in Alaska in August.

During this same period the Korean War had begun and the new ADC, while not in a panic, was certainly becoming apprehensive about gaining air defense interceptors. They had already lost the 4th Fighter-Interceptor Group to the Far East Air Force for duty in Korea, and were about to lose at least one squadron of F-94s for service in Japan. The antiquated F-82F all-weather Twin Mustang had already left their inventory, and the forecasted F-89 schedule was falling further and further behind.

In addition, the USAF decided that only the first eighteen of the contracted for F-89s would be designated as F-89As,

"Hawkeye" of the 74th FIS at Thule AB displays its wingtip rocket armament. -A/2c Menard

A 321st FIS F-89D with a good close-up view of its combination fuel and wingtip rocket armament system. The 321st used a 3, 2, 1 star pattern as part of their motif. -USAF

as these would have their now identified stabilizer buffet flutter problems artificially controlled by external balance weights, called "horns," or "ice tongs," after their appearance. None of these would ever be considered available for assignment to actual combat units in this configuration. The continuance of production of these F-89As was authorized in the Fall of 1950 but problems encountered with the substituted J35-A-21 engines throwing their turbine blades ("buckets") brought about the grounding of the ten aircraft in October that Northrop had available to them for flight tests.

In November 1950, John Northrop met with Air Force Chief of Staff Hoyt Vandenberg and his high ranking subordinates and Northrop was informed that solutions to the encountered tail flutter and shimmying of the aircraft's aft section had to be cured or the USAF would seek other sources for their interceptors. Northrop was given until January 1951 to find the solutions, and in the meantime aircraft construction was stopped. This declaration was particularly painful to Northrop as they had recently lost their contract for the RB-49 flying wing reconnaissance bomber and the long-range outlook for the company was bleak without the F-89 contract.

The grounding order was lifted in January 1951 and the USAF accepted 49-2433 and -2434 during the month. Of these first four accepted examples, three would have the six 20mm T-31 (M-24) cannon armament of the future F-89B and C versions, while -2434 would be used by Northrop to install and evaluate the Martin Aircraft Corporation D-4 cannon turret. At this time it was hoped that this particular turret would prove feasible as the armament system for the F-89.

Only eleven examples of the contracted for forty-eight F-89As were delivered to the USAF as such, and four of these, 49-2424, -2439, -2440, and -2441 would be modified to the first F-89B-1s. Consequently none of the F-89As per se were

ever utilized beyond development and suitability testing. Three of the first F-89As were dispatched to the Air Force Flight Test Center, AFFTC, at Muroc to begin accelerated service tests, ASTs. These were 49-2436, -2437, and -2438, and they were assigned to the 2759th Flight Test Group. Captain Arthur Murry was the Project Officer. Further accelerated tests would not be concluded until July 1951, by then being conducted by the 3077th Experimental Group at Edwards, under Flight Test Division Project 51-F-8.

Of the four F-89As modified to F-89B-1s, -4924 would remain in service as an experimental airframe and would eventually revert back to being redesignated as an EF-89A (the "E" signifying "Exempt from Technical Order criteria" at that time, and not Electronic, as it does today). F-89As -2439 and -2440 would be assigned to the 78th Fighter Interceptor Wing at Hamilton AFB and -2441 to the 128th FIW at Truax AFB, all as ground instructional aircraft.

The next seven examples of what had originally been a part of the F-89A contract became F-89B-5s, 49-2442/-2448. These aircraft also initially became instructional aircraft or were utilized in further development tests. Eventually they would, however, be assigned to Air National Guard squadrons dedicated to ADC duties.

Beginning with the series 49-2449 through -2478 the F-89Bs were either -10s or -15s and these aircraft completed the initial contract for the forty-eight aircraft. The later F-89Bs were equipped with Lear F-5 autopilots, for which William "Bill" Lear received the Collier Trophy for its development in 1949. Also installed was the Sperry Zero Reader, "which combined the functions of a gyro horizon, directional gyro, magnetic compass, sensitive altimeter and cross-pointer indicator." A fan marker beacon receiver was added for Instrument Landing System (ILS) approaches, and the cockpit's lighting was improved. All of this required navigational equipment would make the Scorpion all-weather capable.

The first of the F-89B-10s was made available to the USAF on February 2, 1951, and accepted that same day but it was retained by Northrop for further use in test programs until May 1953. The third of this series, -2451, was assigned to the 83rd Fighter Interceptor Squadron at Hamilton AFB as the first Scorpion to actually be assigned to an operational squadron as an interceptor, under Project ADC-1PF-496. The last of this project's F-89s being delivered to the Air Defense Command on November 29, 1951, -2477. The last actual B model, -2478, was assigned to Wright-Patterson AFB under Project ARD-2F-257 at the end of November.

The first F-89Bs initially came equipped with Allison J35-A-21 engines, and then were upgraded to -21As that produced 5,200 pounds static thrust at 100% military power, or 6,800 pounds with the afterburner in operation. Finally these examples were reequipped with J-35A-47s.

Northrop had retained -2463 under Air Force Contract 1817, Project AMC-1PF-322, for use in developing the first YF-89D. First flown on October 23, 1951, it was lost two years later, almost to the day, in a crash landing at Edwards AFB.

One year to the exact date of the delivery of the first F-89A came the acceptance by the USAF of the first F-89C, 50-741, although the first batch of F-89C-1s were not actually delivered until the middle of October when 50-743 went to first Eglin AFB, and then to Ladd AFB for cold weather testing and climatic evaluation of its systems.

The newer F-89C differed little from the previous models in external appearance, except for the bulbous installation of a Stewart-Warner engine purge generator on its right engine nacelle. This item was utilized to purge the fuel system with inert gases to prevent an explosion in the fuel cells by residue vapors. (Some sources state that the first forty examples still had the elevator mass-balance "horns." This is erroneous.) Internal mass-balance weights replaced the previous "horns," and these were soon retrofitted to surviving F-89A/Bs. The F-89C wingtip fuel tanks were fitted with three inch dump valves to jettison internal fuel in the event of an emergency, as equipped in the Navy's Grumman F9F Panther.

The first flight of the F-89C was on September 18, although it had been accepted by the USAF on the 11th. Deliveries to operational interceptor squadrons of the F-89C commenced on November 16, 1951, with 50-746 being flown to the 78th Fighter Interceptor Wing at Hamilton AFB. The 78th FIW actually received only one other C model before the Wing switched back to F-84s and F-86s, and thus they never became operational with this particular Scorpion version.

The primary recipient of the early F-89Cs, the -1, -5, and -10 versions was the 3625th Combat Crew Training Wing at Tyndall AFB, FL. They commenced receiving them in December for aircrew instruction. The majority of these remained at Tyndall AFB until December 1953/January 1954 when they were reassigned to either the 61st Fighter Interceptor Squadron at Ernest Harmon AB, Newfoundland, or Elmendorf AFB, Alaska, and the 65th FIS. The 176th FIS at Truax AFB, Wisconsin, became the first actually operational recipient of the F-89C-10 on February 8, 1952, when they obtained 50-769 as their first mission Scorpion. These -10 models were

equipped with the improved Allison J-35A-21A engines. Later blocks, -15 through -30, would have J35-A-33 engines, and then blocks -35/-40 received J35-A-33As that produced 7,400 pounds thrust in afterburner.

On January 31, 1952, the Air Defense Command entered a request to Northrop for the development of a nuclear armed interceptor. This would eventually evolve into the F-89J.

On February 25, 1952, the first incident of the new F-89Cs shedding their wings occurred. By September 15 there would be five more of these catastrophes, and then the entire F-89 fleet was grounded. As these incidents were occurring, Northrop was in the process of delivering F-89Cs to the 74th FIS at Presque Isle AFB, Maine, yet by the end of March only nineteen of their authorized twenty-six interceptors had been delivered and further deliveries were curtailed as a result of the investigation of the February 25 incident.

After initially determining that the aforementioned incident was brought on by pilot induced over-stressing of the airframe, the F-89s were released for deliveries again, with limitations upon speeds and G forces permitted. Still, by the end of June, only three more Scorpions were accepted by the ADC. In an attempt to equip the newly activated 433rd FIS at Truax AFB (the renumbered "replacement" squadron for the 176th FIS), some of the 74th FIS F-89s were shuffled to Wisconsin.

Ten of the next F-89Cs were slated for the 27th FIS at Griffiss AFB, New York, who were flying F-86As at the time, but production delays got in the way of this transition program. The 27th FIS received the necessary ground handling equipment, spare parts, commenced classroom training, and received a half dozen Scorpions in July. Their losing one at the International Aviation Exhibition at Detroit helped bring about the Air Force grounding of the F-89 once again and the 27th FIS never became combat ready with the F-89. They continued flying the Sabres they still had on hand until January 1954 when they switched to F-94C Starfires.

Two 74th FIS F-89Cs were lost to catastrophic wing failures, one on July 18 and the other on September 22. These incidents brought about the grounding of the Scorpion on September 25, as mentioned earlier. In the meantime, all of ADC's operational F-89Bs were being returned to Northrop for structural and engine improvements, which would bring them up to F-89C standards.

In October 1952 the ADC expressed interest in the McDonnell F-101, currently in development for the Strategic Air Command as a long-range escort fighter, and for the Tactical Air Command as a fighter bomber. This was brought about by the delays in Convair's F-102 program and all of the problems associated with the F-89. In April 1953 ADC gave a go-ahead to McDonnell to develop a version of the F-101 as an interceptor.

In November 1952 Northrop commenced their redesign of the F-89. As this would involve considerable time and effort, Northrop concentrated upon the aircraft that they actually had on hand at their Hawthorne plant. The major modifi-

Awaiting its acceptance test flight and bearing Northrop's factory markings, F-89D 51-415. The center portion of the wingtip fuel tanks held 308 gallons of fuel. -Esposito Collection

54-267 displays its trapeze mounted Falcon missiles. After last serving with the 123rd FIS it became a museum piece at the Oregon Museum of Science at Portland. -Isham Collection

cations involved a "beefing-up" of the main wing spar and the addition of stabilizing fins to the wingtip fuel tanks, which alleviated any twisting motion to the wing while under a high G stress factor. Those aircraft that were assigned to squadrons remained with them during this period, on standby combat alert status, just in case they might actually be called upon for air defense duties. Engines were run and systems were checked, but they were not permitted to be flown.

In January 1953 those aircraft assigned to squadrons started to be returned for modification. These were flown by Northrop pilots to the Ogden AFB, Utah, Air Material Command Area or Hawthorne for the necessary airframe changes. Headquarters ADC would not permit their own pilots to ferry these aircraft back to the contractors' plants. Also at this time the ADC specified that they would only accept back the modified F-89C, so the USAF programmed the reworked F-89Bs for service in Alaska, but the commander of the Alaskan Air Command, Lt. General George Cheson, also refused to accept them. As a result of this and other incurred delays, by the end of June 1953 the ADC had only thirty-six F-89Cs back in their inventory and Northrop was stuck with the unwanted F-89Bs for the duration.

The complete redesign of the Scorpion's wing cost the taxpayers some $17 million and the delays that the modifications to these early aircraft required meant that it would not be until January 1954 before the reworked aircraft were available once again. By June 1954 ADC had only three squadrons equipped with thirty-nine F-89Cs between them, the 57th FIS at Presque Isle AFB having been activated in March. By the end of the year, however, the ADC would have rid themselves of the troublesome F-89C by transferring the 57th FIS to Iceland, the 74th FIS to the Northeast Air Command, and the 433rd FIS to the Alaskan Air Command. By the end of Fiscal Year 1953 (June 30, 1953) the USAF had accepted all of the remaining F-89Cs, for a total of 182 examples. Yet by the end of 1954, all of these Scorpions were in obsolescent and were reassigned to the Air National Guard.

The F-89D marked the major change in the F-89 that, as with the F-86D and F-94C, its armament consisted solely of rockets. Northrop had commenced the rework of F-89B-15 49-2463 under USAF Contract 1817 and Project AMC-1PF-322 as it came off their production line and it became designated as the YF-89D. Accepted by the USAF on September 28, 1951, it was delivered to Edwards AFB and made its maiden flight on October 23 with Northrop test pilot Ray Tenhoff as pilot. Its first flight took place just a month after the first flight of the F-89C.

The first flight of the production F-89D model, 51-400, was on January 10, 1953, and the first two examples of the new F-89D were delivered in June. The obvious differences from the previous models were the enlarged 308 gallon wingtip fuel tanks that were constructed in three sections, the center and aft sections containing fuel, while the nose portion contained fifty-two 2.75" folding fin aircraft rockets, FFARs. This forward section was separated by stand-offs, which permitted the rocket's exhaust gases to escape and the heat to be drafted away from the fuel tank portion. Additionally, the 20mm cannons were replaced in a extended nose section by a 262 gallon fuel tank, which also replaced ballast that was required in the earlier models. The new J-35-A-33 engines that were installed had improved afterburners for better thrust at high altitudes, and an improved E-6 fire control system, FCS, was integrated with the F-5 autopilot (later an E-11), the AN/APG-40 radar system and the AN/APA-84 rocket ballistics computer.

These early F-89Ds also fell under the USAF's grounding order, and it was not until November 1953 that the aircraft actually returned to mass production, as Northrop continued to concentrate upon reworking the earlier models and had virtually shut down their production line in the meantime to do so. By November 1953 the USAF had only accepted five F-89Ds, while Northrop had 120 examples available and sitting on their ramp. By the time the backlog had been resolved by the modifications the USAF demanded and the necessary FCSs received by subcontractors, 170 F-89Ds had been produced, but 165 of this number had been delayed up to a year in acceptance.

On January 7, 1954, the 18th FIS at Minneapolis-St. Paul International Airport, Minnesota, received their first F-89D.

The 438th FIS at Kinross AFB, Michigan, and the 497th FIS at Portland, Oregon, followed in deliveries the first half of the year. In September the 18th FIS was transferred to the Alaskan Air Command, and was replaced by the 337th FIS. And by the end of 1954 the 82nd and 318th FISs at Presque Isle AFB had re-equipped with F-89Ds after returning from Greenland and Newfoundland with F-94Bs that were to be turned over to the ANG. Thus beginning calendar year 1955, the ADC had only five F-89Ds squadrons.

Unfortunately, these rocket armed Scorpion squadrons could not be considered as combat ready, as most of the aircraft still lacked the improved E-6 FCSs and E-11 autopilots, both of these items also being in heavy demand for use in the F-86D and F-94C. Those aircraft that were fitted with the E-11 autopilot were limited to only Mach .75 when it was in use, as it was found to lack stability under high speed conditions.

The early F-89D, while touted as the fighter of the future by many, still suffered from many of the shortcomings of its predecessor versions. The wing was still deemed as not as robust as it should have been, and the interceptor was "placarded" to 425 mph below 25,000 feet and was limited to the number of Gs (5) the pilot could induce upon it. The engines suffered a "power droop" above 30,000 feet and reduced its ability to gain either additional altitude or speed above this altitude, which definitely reduced its effectiveness. As an interceptor, it was considered capable of challenging the B-29/B-50 series, but not the jet propelled B-47, as it could not get as high as the Stratojet, and with the restrictions placed upon it, it was not fast enough to catch one in a tail chase.

The rocket pods themselves began to suffer from unforeseen problems. Sometimes a rocket launching tube would collapse when a rocket was fired, which would cause a minor explosion within the pod and cause curtailment of further firing. There was no real danger to the aircraft or crew when this occurred, but the situation made the F-89D hardly effective as a interceptor. Another problem was that often after three or four rockets had been fired from a tube, residue from the firing caused the pods to suffer extensive corrosion damage, and the forward portion of the tip tank pod would have to be replaced or rebuilt. Eventually "thick walled" rocket launching tubes were retrofitted as replacements for the weaker tubes.

Of the 682 F-89D examples obtained, 332 would remain as F-89Ds, while 350 from the later block series, D-35 through D-70, were later returned to Northrop where they were modified to become the F-89J. These Js did have the E-9 FCS installed, an improved version of the E-4 system, and also provisions for carrying both the GAR-1 Falcon "semi-active radar-seeker" missile and the nuclear Genie rocket. (The Falcon was originally known as the XF-98 and marked the departure, for the first time, of identifying an unmanned missile as a fighter type. The XF-99 Bomarc missile was the second such identification, and then the USAF returned to manned fighters in the series with the F-100 Super Sabre.)

One hundred fifty-six F-89Hs were procured under contract AF33(600)-26294.. The armament system consisted of the E-9 FCS and three Falcon missiles mounted upon trapezes installed in each modified tiptank, along with twenty-one 2.75 folding fin rockets. The Hughes Aircraft Corporation finally was able to get the E-9 FCS into mass production on May 1, 1955, and in July came the first firing of the improved GAR-3, an advanced version of the Falcon that would become the aircraft's standard armament.

In March 1955 McDonnell received a Letter Contract to proceed with modifications necessary to convert their F-101 to an interceptor. The new aircraft would be the F-101B Voodoo, and its first flight took place on March 27, 1957.

This new F-101, in all versions suffered almost as many teething problems as the F-89, with the exception of the airframe structural failures. Finally, on January 5, 1959 ADC's 60th FIS at Otis AFB became the first ADC squadron to transition from F-94Cs to F-101Bs. Eventually about half of the F-89 squadrons would receive F-101Bs as replacements.

The first flight of the F-89H was on October 26, 1955, but it was not until March 1956 that the first F-89H was delivered

A "plane Jane" F-89J, as delivered to the 437th FIS at Oxnard AFB, California. Before modification to a F-89J under Project Bell Boy, it served as a D model with the 65th FIS, and later went to the 179th FIS at Duluth, Minnesota, to replace their F-94Cs. -Northrop Grumman Corp.

F-89J 53-2449 of Northrop's Flight Test over Edwards AFB, California, in May 1957. It is carrying four Falcons and two Genies, its standard armament. A camera pod is installed under the interceptor's nose. -Northrop Grumman Corp.

to an operational squadron, the 445th FIS at Wurtsmith AFB, Michigan. This was two years after the original expectation date and only one month ahead of the F-102 Delta Dart's first assignment to an ADC squadron. The F-89H would probably have the shortest operational career of any particular fighter version ever built. The F-89H, although heavier armed, still was underpowered and continued to lack acceleration, rate of climb, and service ceiling. Under combat conditions it could not come even close to intercepting the B-52 Stratofortress that was just becoming operational.

Assigned to nine ADC squadrons, the F-89H became operational with only five of them before they were replaced by F-89Js and relegated to the ANG.

Also in March came Project "Bell Boy," the beginning of the programmed conversion of the later F-89Ds to F-89Js. On March 15 the first of these J models was flown from Palmdale. The new Js (revamped Ds) exchanged their E-6 FCSs for MG-12 FCSs, which was an improved and redesignated E-9 FCS, and this new system permitted the Scorpion to make "snap-up attacks against higher flying targets when the F-89 was in a nose-high climbing attitude." This was in addition to the previous "lead-collision" or "lead pursuit" techniques.

The F-89J was also to be armed with two MB-1 Genie nuclear rockets (designed by Douglas and originally code named "Ding Dong"), in addition to four Falcons. The first airborne firing of the MB-1, later designated as the AIR-2, was on March 8, 1956, from a test F-89D at Holloman AFB, New Mexico. A week later its first firing from a F-89J occurred.

In May 1956 the first flight tests of the F-89J with the MG-12 FCS and the complete armament system took place.

Strangely enough, there was no differential block system utilized to identify the different J models, apparently because the parts were interchangeable. The first thirty-five Js were equipped with the MG-12 FCS, 2.75" F-89D wingtank rocket pods and MB-1 pylons. Numbers thirty-six through one hundred had the MG-12 and provisions for a Fighter Missile System to support the GAR-2 and provisions for GAR-2 pylons. The last series, numbers 101 through 350, had all of the above installed. Thus all Js were to be shipped from Northrop with the F-89D wingtip rocket/fuel tank combination, but the receiving command could specify differently. Regardless, 600 gallon wingtip fuel tanks would be supplied by Northrop at some point. Additionally, although initial equipment was the MB-1 pylons, the interchangeable underwing fuel tank pylons were also to be furnished. In operational practice, the Falcon pylons were removed when it was discovered that the missile became useless after exposure to the elements. (An operational evaluation demonstrated that the Sidewinder missile was more effective than the GAR-2, but the installation of these was determined not to be feasible.)

The combat ceiling on the heavy Js was 40,500' at 39,000 pounds, and only 24,800' at 42,200 pounds gross weight. The all-up gross weight of the F-89J could reach as high as 47,720 pounds when the pylon fuel tanks were installed. The highest Mach attainable was but .82, which was the normal Mach cruise speed for the emerging Boeing 707 and Douglas DC-8 civilian airliners.

In December 1956 the 84th FIS began conversion from F-89Hs to Js, and by January 1957 they were completely re-equipped, while five other ADC squadrons were in the middle of switching from F-89Hs to Js.

On July 19, 1957, a 84th FIS team test fired the first and only detonated nuclear MB-1 Genie at Yucca Flats, Nevada (of which more will be described later). A week later the GAR-2A Falcon was successfully tested.

Production of the Scorpion was terminated in March 1956, but modification to existing airframes from Ds to Js continued for two more years. With this final program being completed two weeks ahead of schedule, it was, unfortunately, about the only time during the entire F-89 program that one was accomplished within its original time parameters.

On June 30, 1958, the ADC had 342 F-89s in its inventory, with 231 considered combat ready, their highest number of combat ready Scorpions. All were either Hs or Js with the exception of the 460th FIS at Portland that still had Ds. (These figures not including the 57th FIS in Iceland.)

In late 1958 those remaining early F-89Ds were phased out of ADC's inventory and went into service with the ANG, which in turn phased out their by now ancient F-89Cs. The F-89H also started going to the ANG during this time frame, with the 123rd FIS at Portland receiving the first batch having been allocated to the ANG the previous November. They were all removed from ADC's inventory by September 1959. In December 1960 the F-89J began leaving ADC's fleet for duty with the ANG, being replaced by the F-101 and the F-106. Briefly in 1962 the F-89D would return to ADC when the last operational USAF squadron so equipped, the 57th FIS, was transferred to their control from the Military Air Transport Service in Iceland, and these would be replaced by F-102s.

Chapter Two: The Air Defense Command

To enhance one's understanding of the Scorpion's assignment to the Air Defense Command (ADC), it is helpful to have an idea of the composition of the ADC itself during the F-89 era.

During the ten year period from 1951-1961 when the F-89 was to be a major tool in ADC's inventory, the ADC was divided into three major areas in its role of defending the contiguous United States. The Eastern Air Defense Force, EADF, Central Air Defense Force, CADF, and Western Air Defense Force, WADF, (Pronounced ee-daff, etc.). Each of these Air Defense Forces was further broken down into Air Divisions, Air Defense Wings, and/or Air Defense Groups.

Each Air Division, AD, was composed of a chain of command to include at least one Air Defense Wing, ADW, or Air Defense Group, ADG, depending upon the size of the geographical area to be covered. Each of these units were then further composed of their own Headquarters Squadron and also included Aircraft Control and Warning, AC&W, squadrons and associated radar sites; assigned and reporting Ground Observer Corps, GOC, units; and of course, dedicated fighter-interceptor squadrons, FIS(s). The primary assigned fighter squadron was normally colocated with the headquarters of the controlling Air Division, Wing or Group, as was the controlling AC&W site.

During the early portion of the ADC history the GOC's visual observation of aircraft was a primary method of detection, as the radar sites were few and limited to densely populated areas of the United States. The GOC observation post gave their observation of an aircraft to a "filter center" which then established a manual track of the aircraft on a plotting board and then forwarded this track to their nearest AC&W site for further radar identification, tracking, and possible interception.

In 1948 General Tooey Spaatz ordered ADC to establish an air defense system in the northeast and northwest portions of the United States, as well as within the existing Alaskan Air Command (which was purely a tactical force at the time). This came about as one of the results of the communist takeover in Czechoslovakia and the Berlin Blockade situations. Actually, preplanning for the construction of required radar sites had commenced in 1947 with a proposed cost of close to $400 million for the establishment of 374 radar sites in the United States and 37 more in Alaska. Political procrastination delayed and reduced the funding for the implementation of this program, known as "Supremacy," until 1949, and then the watered-down program only provided funding for seventy-five sites and ten control centers, and their activation was not scheduled for completion until 1952.

These new AC&W sites were primarily to be equipped with either WWII surplus equipment or equipment already on order, but no funding was allocated for the design of new detection methodology. The new sites would be to provide radar coverage in the Northeast, Northwest, California, and the atomic energy plant at Albuquerque, New Mexico. This reduced program was appropriately identified as "Lash-up."

By mid-1950, a year after Russia had exploded its first atomic device, and just after the Korean Conflict had started, only forty-four of these radar sites had been completed. On January 1, 1951, the ADC, which had been an "operational command" subordinate to the Continental Air Command since September 1949, became an independent command once again. This change finally brought in new funding dedicated to air defense and expansion of the system.

In February 1950 the Ground Observer Corps was authorized by the USAF. The GOC was to be composed of a limited number of Air Force personnel and 25,000 civilian observation posts to fill in the blank spots in radar coverage. They would operate in conjunction with a similar program already underway in Canada. Unfortunately, by 1957 the GOC had only two-thirds of this number of observation posts active, primarily due to civilian apathy, although at one time the GOC had 350,000 volunteers manning their observation posts and filter centers.

50-779, a F-89C-15, started its service life with the 176th FIS on March 18, 1952, and then went to the 433rd FIS on November 1 when the 433rd was activated and obtained the assets of the 176th. After undergoing the wing strengthening modifications, it was returned to the 433rd, by then in Alaska, and later in its life was assigned to the 126th FIS at Milwaukee, Wisconsin. -Esposito

OPPOSITE: 50-777 was transferred to the 433rd FIS from the 176th FIS when they were activated at Truax AFB, Wisconsin, on November 1, 1952. Two months later it was refurbished and transferred to the 65th FIS in Alaska and on October 29, 1953, it was lost in a crash, with the pilot ejecting and the RO being killed. -W. J. Balogh, Sr.

A factory-fresh F-89C as delivered to the 57th FIS at Presque Isle AFB. It finished out its career with Michigan's 171st FIS. -W. J. Balogh, Sr.

51-5855 was the second from the last F-89C-40. It was assigned to the 433rd FIS at Truax AFB, now Truax Air National Guard Base, the "military" side of the Dane County Regional Airport. The scorpion insignia on the vertical stabilizer was an unapproved design. -USAF

Also established was the Air Defense Identification Zones, ADIZs, which ringed the United States. Aircraft intending to enter the United States through one of these zones were required to file a flight plan with either the Civil Aeronautics Administration (the forerunner of today's FAA), or the Military Flight Service, a tracking system of military aircraft operated by the Military Air Transport Service (today's Air Mobility Command). Pilots were expected to adhere to their flight plan, or plan on being intercepted and receiving a violation. In all, it was a very antiquated system with little electronic wizardry that was not far removed from the same system that had been utilized during the Battle of Britain a decade earlier.

Joining the air defense system was the US Army Antiaircraft Command, ARAACOM. This command was established on July 1, 1950, and a month later an agreement between the Army and the USAF placed ARAACOM under operational control of ADC. Although slow to be implemented, ARAACOM eventually brought 90 and 120mm antiaircraft cannons, along

with 75mm radar-controlled Skysweeper cannons into the air defense system. By 1957 these were augmented by at least thirteen NIKE short-ranged ground-to-air radar directed guided missile sites near major metropolitan areas.

By 1954 Lashup was functional as an integrated system with ADC radars, ARAACOM emplacements and the GOC in operation. Yet the system was far from complete, as it was full of holes in radar coverage. In January 1954 a gap filler program was authorized, which would add 300 automatic radar feeder sites into the existing system, with their observations being transmitted to the primary site electronically. This would be supplemented by 100 mobile radar sites which would come on line in 1958.

While this was occurring, it was recognized that the existing system would provide little actual early warning of an approaching enemy aircraft. Particularly those that might be coming across the North Pole area, the shortest air route from Russia. In 1951 an agreement with Canada led to the establishment of the Pinetree Line, a series of some thirty radar stations across southern Canada, of which the United States built approximately twenty and Canada the remaining number. This line was reinforced by the Mid-Canada Line, authorized in 1954 by agreement between the two countries, and spanning Canada along the 55th Parallel. These sites were all built by the Canadian government, and would be the first to provide for actual early warning of an approaching aggressor.

Further north, within the Arctic Circle, came the establishment of the Distant Early Warning Line, DEW. This line of radar sites spanned 3,000 miles along the 69th Parallel and linked the radars of the Alaskan Air Command with those of the Northeast Air Command. Actual construction of the DEW Line commenced in early 1955 after months of acrimonious public debate over the envisioned need for such an expensive system. Completed and declared operational on August 1, 1957, an assignment to these frigid and remote locations was viewed with extreme trepidation by USAF radar person-

51-5793 of the 74th FIS at Presque Isle AFB, Maine. The 74th and 57th utilized similar paint schemes, which corresponded to their parent air division's motif. -W. J. Balogh, Sr.

nel, and many of the sites were staffed in part by highly paid civilian personnel in lieu of Airmen.

Two additional early warning radar detection programs were constructed and/or operated to provide advance warning of an enemy aircraft that might be approaching North America from over water instead of over land.

The first of these were USAF and US Navy airborne Lockheed RC-121s and their Navy counterpart, the WV-2 ("Willie Victor"), a military modification of the Constellation airliner. The first of these picket/patrol aircraft commenced providing twenty-four hour airborne radar coverage off both coasts in 1953 and continued to supplement picket ships and Texas Towers well into the 1960s.

The "Texas Towers" were radar sites constructed upon platforms that were similar to floating oil rigs, only they were anchored to the ocean bottom. The first of these, Texas Tower-2, located off Cape Cod on George's Shoal in the Atlantic Ocean, became operational in May 1956. Four more were planned, but only two of these ever became operational, in 1957. They replaced US Navy picket ships that had been in use in a similar role since 1950. On January 15, 1961, TT-4 collapsed during heavy seas with the loss of twenty-eight lives. On March 25, 1963, the towers were decommissioned.

On September 1, 1954, a new command was formed to come under the control of the Joint Chiefs of Staff to oversee the US Army, USAF, and US Navy's participation in air defense. Identified as the Continental Air Defense Command, ConAD, its first commander was General Benjamin W. Chidlaw, who also commanded ADC at the time. General Earle E. Partridge became commander of both the ADC and ConAD on July 20, 1955. On September 12, 1957, ConAD was replaced by NORAD, North American Air Defense Command, a joint endeavor between the United States and Canada. Partridge assumed command of NORAD with Air Vice Marshal William MacBrian as his Canadian deputy, and General Joseph Atkinson became the commander of the ADC portion of NORAD.

A 57th FIS F-89C at Presque Isle AFB prior to their relocation to Iceland. They had obtained it from the 74th FIS to reinforce their compliment of aircraft, and it would later be assigned to the 171st FIS. Note the characteristic F-89C purge generator on the engine nacelle. -via David Menard

Automation finally came to NORAD in early 1958 with the advent of the Semi-Automatic Ground Environment, SAGE, System. This digital tube-type computer system was hardly as sophisticated as today's lap-top, yet it required a huge fortress-like concrete structure to house its electronic equipment and its required cooling system for the electron tubes. (The cost was $8 million for each structure.) All this was the forerunner of modern air defense and evolved into today's air traffic control systems. It finally combined viable range, azimuth, and height finding data together. The SAGE system transmitted automatically to the interceptor the direction and altitude to be flown via Data Link, without the necessity of voice direction while processing and displaying the relative positions of the fighter and the intended target to the

Another new F-89C as assigned to the 57th FIS. This example later went to Wisconsin's 176th FIS to replace their F-51Hs and F-86As. - USAF

A brand new F-89D-20 as delivered to the 438th FIS at Kinross AFB, Michigan. Kinross was renamed Kinchloe AFB in 1959 after Ivan Kinchloe, a Korean War ace and test pilot who lost his life in a F-104 accident. -Sam Sellars

intercept director. The required airborne equipment was tested and certified by F-89s working with MIT's Lincoln Lab and then retrofitted to ADC fighters then in use, such as the F-86D/L, and would become standard equipment on the F-102 and subsequent fighters that were entering the inventory. (See Chapter Six: Test Missions for additional information on these F-89s). The first SAGE site became operational with the 26th Air Division at Hancock AFB, Syracuse, New York, in 1958.

While all of these programs were being implemented within the hierarchy of ADC, other changes were effected to the basic fighter wing structures and their chains of authority.

Back in July of 1947 the USAF experimented with the Hobson Plan, which did away with the traditional three Groups to the Wing configuration and established new Wings to control a specific air field or Air Force Base, with the new Wing headquarters assuming the role of the previous Air Base Unit,

BASUT. These new Wings were strictly administrative and had no heritage of their own, and they and their air base were dedicated to their controlling agency, the Strategic Air Command, MATS or ADC, depending upon the air base's primary role. For example: the 56th Fighter Wing replaced the 146th BASUT at Selfridge AFB, Michigan, with the 56th FW being dedicated to SAC until December 1948, and then the ADC. The 56th Fighter Group was the operational unit with three fighter squadrons flying F-80s, first dedicated as escort fighters, then interceptors. Thus Selfridge was first considered to be a SAC base, then an ADC base. However, if an ADC squadron or group was assigned to an air base under the control of another command, as most of them were, then they were a "tenant" organization. In July 1948 the Hobson Plan was declared feasible and the Wing assignments then became a permanent fixture.

51-11316 was the personal F-89D of Major Forest Parham, the squadron commander of the 438th FIS. In this view he is taking off from Yuma AFB after a 1954 rocketry exercise. -Sam Sellars

Major Parham leads a flight of three 438th FIS F-89Ds over the Upper Peninsula of Michigan. -Sam Sellars

Prior to February 2, 1952, all of ADC's squadrons had been assigned to their original numbered parent fighter group in the traditional three squadrons to the group fashion that had been in use since before WWII. But after this date all of ADC's fighter groups were inactivated and replaced, in designation, by newly activated Air Defense Wings or Groups under this confusing program. For example: Under the new 30th Air Division at Selfridge, the 56th Fighter Wing became the 4708th Defense Wing on February 6, 1952, and then on February 16, 1953, this Wing was inactivated and the 575th Air Defense Group was activated in its place, which then reported directly to the 30th AD. Of the three original squadrons assigned to the 56th FW, the 62nd FIS had moved to O'Hare AFB, Illinois, in August 1950, and they then came

51-11328 of the 438th FIS. She was lost on August 8, 1956 while making a practice GCA approach. The crew was killed. -Sam Sellars

under the control of the newly created 4706th DW in 1952. The 63rd FIS moved to Oscoda AFB, Michigan, in January 1951 and they also came under the control of the 4706th DW, while the 61st FIS remained at Selfridge until July 1953, and during this period they were only interceptor squadron assigned to the new 4708th DW/575th ADG.

Exactly why this was done cannot be determined, as even the ADC historian at the time was not made privy to the reason. It might be surmised that it was a public relations ploy by the Air Force, as "Air Division" certainly sounds more formidable than "Group," not withstanding that most of ADC's original three squadron fighter groups had already been reduced to one or two squadron strength.

Originally, most of these newly created Air Defense Wings or Air Divisions were assigned either two or four digit designations for identification, with the four digit designations being considered temporary. But on February 16, 1953, most of the two digit identifications were changed to three digits, and the four digit identifiers were revised to either two or three. Again the "why for" this change eluded ADC's historian.

Following these two changes came "Project Arrow," which did have a modicum of logic behind it. However, "Arrow" created even more of a massive headache for unit and other historians. Project Arrow was implemented on August 18, 1955, in an attempt to re-establish ADC's fighter squadron lineage back with their original WWII parent fighter groups. At this time most of the newer three digit fighter groups were inactivated and replaced in designation by those of the recreated fighter groups, and an attempt was made to place the new group's number back in its original location.

A massive shuffle of squadron designations then took place as squadrons were relocated "Without Personnel and Equipment," WOPE, overnight in this attempt to realign their heritage with that of their original group—a situation that created a real challenge to those who attempted to follow a unit's history, lineage and honors. (Heritage and lineage policy is based upon a unit's number and age, and not on those people who gave the unit recognition to begin with. People come and go, while the unit endures.) Once again the 56th FG was reactivated, this time at O'Hare IAP, Illinois, as an example of this, and they regained the 62nd and 63rd Fighter Squadrons, but the "new" 63rd FIS was actually the "old" 42nd FIS at O'Hare, as the old 42nd FIS went to Pittsburgh under Project Arrow to replace the 71st FIS, which then went to Selfridge AFB to rejoin the reactivated 1st Fighter Interceptor Group and replace the 13th FIS in designation, which in turn was relocated to Sioux City, Iowa. This basically was the organizational structure of ADC that was in place during ADC's Scorpion era.

The first assignment of the F-89 to an operational unit was on June 21, 1951, when the fourth F-89B-10NO, 49-2452, and three others were delivered to the 78th Fighter Interceptor Wing at Hamilton AFB, California, under Project ADC 1PF-496. As might be expected, there was celebration by the "Norcrafters" that had been working on the F-89s for

Major Parham and M/Sgt. Rhodes, line Chief of the 438th FIS. The "Ruthless Ruth" name is taken from the Parrymore poem "The Ballad of Yukon Jake." -Sam Sellars

"The Challenger" was the personal F-89 of Captain Hustad and Lt. Ricks for participation in the 1954 Allison Trophy Race. -Pete Bowers via David Menard

so long, and the Air Force also did their part by sending some high ranking pilots to the plant to accept these first interceptors. Colonel Bryan O'Neill, commanding officer of Hamilton AFB, led the flight back with Colonel Jack Hayes, commanding officer of the 78th Fighter Interceptor Group, Group operations officer Lt. Colonel C. L. Van Etten, and Lt Colonel Phillip Joyal, commanding officer of the 84th Fighter Interceptor Squadron, composing the remainder of the flight. Before June was over five more F-89Bs were delivered from Northrop, and after acceptance checks, these fighters were assigned to either the 83rd or 84th Fighter Interceptor Squadrons to replace their F-84Ds. The Wing's third squadron, the 82nd FIS, would continue with the Thunderjet, and they would relocate to Larson AFB, Washington, in February 1952 to convert to F-94Bs.

1954 Allison Trophy winners Sam Sellars and (now) California Congressman Pete Knight. This race might be considered as rigged, as all four competitors were flying Allison powered F-89s. -Sam Sellars

The initial reception of the Scorpion was good, as the pilots were impressed that it had more "get up and go" than the ground loving Thunderjet, but of course, as technology improved fighters over the next decade, the F-89 became known as a ground lover, too, as it became noted for its lack of acceleration and slow rate of climb in comparison to newer aircraft.

In November 1951 the 78th FIW began receiving the first F-89C-1s. On February 2, 1952, the 78th FIW was inactivated and replaced in designation by the 4702nd Air Defense Wing, with Colonel Hayes continuing in position as Wing Commander. In late April 1952 the 83rd FIS received a Warning Order for a move to Paine AFB, Washington, and on May 1 their eleven assigned F-89 B's and C's were turned over to the 84th FIS, which gave the 84th a total of thirty-five Scorpions. On July 27 the 83rd FIS left for Paine to fly first F-84s, then F-86Ds. Yet by this time the 84th FIS was already running an off again, on again operation with their F-89s, as F-86Fs had started to arrive in June to replace them. The subject F-89s were soon headed back to Northrop for modification, after which most would be assigned to the 176th FIS.

The 84th FIS replaced their Sabres with F-94Bs in January 1953. On February 16, 1953, the 4702nd ADW was redesignated as the 566th Air Defense Group. In July 1953 the F-94B gave way to the F-94C Starfire, but Scorpions returned to their inventory in the fall of 1955 when they received twenty-six F-89Ds. By this time their parent organization had gone "full circle," as the 566th ADG was redesignated as the 78th FIG on August 18, 1955 under Project Arrow, with the 84th FIS being their sole operational squadron. Colonel Wilton Earle was the commanding officer of the new 78th FIG.

In the spring of 1956 the 84th FIS switched to F-89Hs, which they flew for almost a year before converting to F-89Js in January 1957, being ADC's first F-89J squadron. And it was with the J model that they gained fame in several events. On July 19, 1957, as covered elsewhere, Captains Eric Hutchinson and Radar Observer Albert Barbee fired the first

438th FIS alert hangers at Kinchloe AFB. These "barns" were completely self-contained installations with their own heating plants, mess halls, and sleeping quarters, etc. -Sam Sellars

air-to-air live atomic weapon, for which they each received the Distinguished Flying Cross. In September 1958 the 84th FIS deployed to Vincent AFB, where they broke all previous records in air-to-air rocketry. This qualified them for ADC's first William Tell meet at Tyndall AFB the following month, where they placed third in firing in an exercise that was not decided until the last day's events had been tallied. Colonel Cueleers, the squadron commander, also tied for individual honors. On April 21, 1959, the first of the new supersonic VooDoos arrived, and on August 26 the 84th FIS was operational with F-101s.

The 176th Fighter Squadron at Truax Field, Madison, Wisconsin (today the military side of the Dane County Regional Airport), had been activated into Federal Service on February 1, 1952 as a part of the call-up of selected Air National Guard squadrons during the Korean Conflict. Major

Oliver Ryerson was their squadron commander at the time, and they were flying a limited number of F-51Ds, having transferred most of their Mustangs back to the regular Air Force for service in Korea. As was the case with the majority of the Federalized ANG squadrons with an air defense commitment, they remained at their home base. (Whereas those with a tactical commitment were transferred to other Air Force bases.)

Although it is generally believed that the 176th FIS was the first operational F-89A squadron, this was not exactly the situation. The first F-89 example received, 49-2441, was actually one of the first As that had been modified to B configuration on Northrop's production line. This particular example was assigned to the squadron's parent 128th Fighter Interceptor Wing for service as an instructional airframe on November 14, 1951, and it did not reach the 176th FIS until February 6, 1952. Two days later the first of the squadron's compliment of F-89Cs arrived, and by March 21 they had a dozen Scorpions on their Truax ramp.

The 176th FIS's relationship with the F-89C was quite limited, as all of their aircraft were grounded on September 25. When their period of active duty with the USAF was over and they returned to State Control, on October 31, 1952, their ground-bound Scorpions were transferred to the 433rd FIS. At this time the 176th FIS received F-51Hs, which they flew with an ADC commitment until October 1954, with some F-86As being brought in with the intention of phasing out the Mustangs in favor of Sabres, but this was an action that was never completed.

Scorpions would replace the mixed bag of Mustangs and Sabres of the 176th FIS in October 1954, and this period is covered in Chapter Four: The Air National Guard.

The 433rd FIS, having been activated at Truax Field on November 1, 1952, to replace the 176th FIS, obviously got

At Paine Field, Oregon, 51-11441 of the 497th FIS. Under Project Arrow in August 1955 the 497th became a F-86D squadron at Geiger Field, Washington, and the "old" 497th was redesignated at the 460th FIS. -via David Menard

51-11370 of the 497th FIS over the wilds of Oregon. -USAF via Stammer

off to a difficult start, as all of their aircraft were grounded for the first six weeks of their history. In fact, by the end of the year they possessed but a dozen F-89Cs, and none of these were "combat ready." At the time of activation, Lt. Colonel Victor Milner was squadron commander, while Major John Moutier was Executive Officer. The first flight commanders were Majors Samuel Denmark and John Rogers.

The 433rd FIS was assigned to the 31st Air Division, which was also a newly activated unit headquartered at Truax that likewise took control over the newly activated 11th and 18th FIS's in Minnesota. (The 31st AD would be redesignated as the 520th Air Defense Group on February 16, 1953). The 433rd FIS began to switch to F-94Bs brought in from the Air Training Command in Florida as replacement interceptors on January 7, 1953, while their Scorpions were being returned to Northrop for refurbishment. By the end of June they still had five F-94s remaining but they had regained their dozen F-89Cs, with five of these finally being considered as combat ready. On July 20, 1954, the 433rd FIS was transferred from Truax to Ladd AFB, Alaska, and assigned to the Alaskan Air Command.

In New England the first assignments of the F-89C were intended for two of the five squadrons assigned to the 4711st Air Defense Wing, EADF, which was then under the command of Colonel Norval Heath. The 4711th ADW was one of the larger ADWs, being composed of two ANG squadrons, flying F-51Ds and F-80Cs, while three regular USAF squadrons were flying F-86A and Es.

The first of these squadrons to be re-equipped with F-89Cs was the 74th FIS at Presque Isle AFB, Maine. Major Richard Crutcher was their commanding officer. Their first Scorpion received was a B model that was assigned for maintenance instruction in April 1952, which was followed by de-

In 1955 the 58th FIS converted from F-94Cs to F-89Ds. This example, "all buttoned up," with safety pin and gust locks installed, was placed on display at the National Aircraft Show, Philadelphia, Pennsylvania, in September 1955. -USAF

livery of the first three of the allocated compliment of F-89Cs on June 15.

Three days later, on June 18, the first indicator of the shortcomings of the Scorpion occurred when a wing folded on one of these aircraft. Captain Al Breitkrcutz and 1st Lt. Ray Moony were killed. Ray Moony had been the first Radar Observer to obtain a kill with the 6th Night Fighter Squadron during WWII, and he had three more kills during that war. He had started out as a Technical Sergeant and had risen through the ranks to become an officer. At first the cause for the loss was believed to be pilot induced, through pulling far more Gs than the aircraft had been designed for.

By the end of July the 74th FIS had thirteen F-89s assigned and transition training continued, with the squadron standing alert with their F-86s until the task was accomplished. But on September 22, Captain Samuel Nelson and R/O 2nd Lt. Conway Roberts had another wing failure occur. A loud "crack" was heard and the wing started to fold up over their canopy. Roberts ejected successfully, but Nelson's seat failed to fire and he narrowly escaped from the aircraft by bailing out manually before it crashed. This accident brought about the fleet-wide grounding of the F-89 on September 25.

The 74th FIS borrowed back F-86As from other squadrons to continue their alert commitment and held their F-89s in a combat alert readiness status, in the event that they might have to be flown in an actual war, until they were relieved from their alert status on December 12. At this time they commenced transition to F-94Bs. The 74th FIS then became operational with the F-94 until June 1953 when the first of eight reworked F-89s were returned to them from Northrop and the squadron actually became operational with the Scorpion.

On December 15, 1953, the 74th FIS lost another Scorpion at Limestone AFB, Maine (later Loring AFB). 2nd Lt.'s

The 11th FIS was another ADC squadron that had been created to replace an ANG squadron that was being released from Federal control during the Korean War emergency. They only flew the F-89 for a short period. In early 1955 they had begun conversion from F-86Ds to F-89Ds, but by the Fall of 1956 they had switched to F-102As. -via Jim Wogstad

Grady Breland and R/O Bill Hill were trying to get into Limestone in instrument weather, but missed the runway and crashed a mile north-northwest of the airfield. The exact cause for this loss was never determined, but IFR weather and the crew's inexperience was a primary factor.

In January 1954 a Warning Order was received informing the 74th FIS of an impending transfer to Greenland and their compliment of F-89s was increased to seventeen. They would also gain additional personnel via transfer from the 57th FIS, which was also at Presque Isle AFB, to increase their manpower.

On August 6 the movement to Thule Air Base began via MATS C-54s and C-124s. The F-89s staged through Goose Bay, Bluie West 1, Narsarssuak, and then Bluie West 8, Sondrestrom. On August 9 Major Crutcher landed the first F-89 north of the Arctic Circle. Effective August 21 the 74th FIS was thus reassigned from ADC to the North East Air Command, but due to weather and other problems, the last 74th FIS F-89 did not land at Thule until August 25. (As this movement was taking place, the 318th FIS was in the process of returning to the United States from Thule with F-94Bs. The F-94s would be transferred to the Air National Guard, and the 318th FIS would replace the 74th FIS at Presque Isle with F-89Ds).

The 27th FIS was the second 4711th ADW fighter squadron to receive the F-89C. They were stationed at Griffiss AFB, Rome, New York, under the command of Lt. Colonel Benjamin Emmert. Emmert had just returned from Korea, and he had one MiG 15 to his credit. They received their first Scorpion in July 1952, flown in by J. J. Quinn.

As the 27th FIS was also flying F-86As at the time, they had problems in obtaining qualified Radar Observers as well. Their newly assigned R/Os were all young officers that were arriving from Moody AFB, where they had ground instruction in radar and interception techniques, but little actual practice, as Moody's F-89Bs were all grounded and opportunity for practical airborne experience was limited to available backseat time in F-94s that had to be shared with that school. Thus

The 58th FIS had switched to F-89Hs in 1956, and then to F-89Js in 1957. -Ron Picciani

transition into the new Scorpion was erratic at best. Each pilot was required to make three solo flights in the F-89 before he could even take a R/O up with him.

Right after the first crews became qualified in the F-89, a request came in to the 27th FIS for them to provide two Scorpions for aerial and ground display at the International Aviation Exhibition at Wayne County Airport, Detroit, Michigan, on Labor Day weekend. Major Donald Adams and R/O Edward Kelly were selected to lead the flight, while John Recheir and R/O Captain Thomas Myslicki would fly the second aircraft.

Towards the conclusion of the first day of the exhibition, on Saturday, August 30, the two Scorpions took off and then made a descending high-speed low-pass over the airport. As fortune had it, Adams missed his run-in point to pass in front of the crowded bleachers, and as the F-89s started a rolling pull-out behind the crowds, the Scorpion flown by Adams snapped its left wing off at the root. The F-89 rolled violently

53-2568 of the 58th FIS. This Scorpion came to its demise on July 2, 1956, when its pilot landed too close to the side of the runway and collapsed its landing gear, resulting it its having to be salvaged. -Tom Cuddy

A 58th FIS F-89J with its new paint scheme on a visit to Philadelphia, Pennsylvania, in 1958. Note that its "blow-in" doors are open during taxi operations. -Esposito

A 58th FIS F-89J. The 58th relocated to Walker AFB, New Mexico, in August 1959 and were inactivated in December 1960. -Tom Cuddy

and its aft section broke away just behind the afterburners, and the F-89 cartwheeled into the ground. Adams, who was the squadron operations officer and had 6.5 MiG kills when he was the commanding officer of the 16th FIS in Korea, and Kelly were both fatally injured. If they had made their pass as intended the wreckage would have plummeted into the spectators and surely would have resulted in a massive number of casualties, as it was, only three on the ground were injured.

As all F-89s were grounded four weeks later, the 27th FIS never did become operational with them, although they did keep them in readiness at Griffiss until the following March when they finally had their turn at being returned to Northrop for rework. The 27th FIS did continue with F-86As until 1954 when the Sabres were replaced by Starfires.

The 57th FIS ("The Black Knights of Aroostook") was activated at Presque Isle AFB on March 27, 1953, and also assigned to the 4711th ADW. The 4711th was now being commanded by Colonel James Beckwith. The newly activated 57th FIS was commanded by Major Claude Hanley, who had previously been the commanding officer of the 26th FIS on Okinawa. (The 26th FIS, as the aforementioned 16th FIS that Adams had commanded, was a part of the 51st FIW. The 16th and 25th FIS's went to Korea in September 1950, while the 26th FIS remained on Okinawa to serve as that Wing's Operational Training Unit. Captain Russell Brown, who scored the first air-to-air jet kill with a F-80 over a MiG 15 in November 1950, and now was serving as operations officer of the 4711th ADW's 37th FIS, had also been a member of the 26th FIS). Captain Robert Staton was transferred from the 27th FIS to the new 57th FIS to serve as their operations officer.

While awaiting delivery of their Scorpions, the 57th FIS R/Os trained in TB-25K Mitchell bombers that had been converted to airborne radar trainers by Hughes Aircraft Corporation. The pilots flew T-6 Texans. Finally, on June 18, Major "Tex" Hanley and 1st Lt. Vernon Burke flew in the first two F-89Cs. By the end of September the squadron had grown to

81 officers, 249 enlisted men, and had twenty-one F-89Cs, along with a T-33A and two TB-25Ks. Also in September they commenced pulling ADC alert duties.

On September 31 the 57th FIS lost their first F-89 and crew when Merle Hroch and R/O 2nd Lt. John Terpinitz "were up leading a two-plane section." After returning to Presque Isle and after their wingman landed, Hroch shot a practice approach, "went around, called for landing instructions." Their F-89 was unheard from again, and it was found inverted in a swamp five miles south of Presque Isle the next morning with its crew dead.

On January 30, 1954, an unusual occurrence for a F-89 brought about the loss of a R/O. Two Scorpions had taken off for a practice mission, with the second one following the first a thousand feet behind in an intrail climbout. Just as they broke out above the clouds, the second Scorpion lost its canopy. The radar operator, 2nd Lt. Robert Kennedy, ejected but his parachute failed to fully open and he was killed. The pilot managed to return and land the F-89 okay, but he was half frozen from the frigid winter wind blasting through his cockpit and had to be helped out of the aircraft.

On March 4 the 57th FIS lost a Scorpion on takeoff from Griffiss AFB, where they had stopped while on a cross-country mission. Their F-89 was seen to climb out slowly while flames were seen emitting from its aft section. Crewed by two pilots, operations officer Captain Staton and 1st Lt. Ernie Neubert, the F-89 hit high tension wires and crashed, and both were killed. Gene Zierden became the squadron's new operations officer.

There is some evidence that the 57th FIS was a "snake bit" squadron while at Presque Isle, for on May 24 they lost another F-89C, but this time with a happier outcome. 1st Lt. Vernon Burke and R/O 2nd Lt. Leroy Vestal took a Scorpion up on a maintenance test flight and lost all of their electrical

54-333 of the 76th FIS. The Falcon rocket armament of the F-89H was not to be fired if there was any fuel remaining in the wingtip tanks, as the stress of the firing would overload the wingtank attachment fittings. -via David Menard

systems. After running out of fuel, they made what was believed to be the first successful double ejection from a F-89. Although they had to walk out of rugged wooded country, both were uninjured.

On October 20, 1954, the first 57th FIS F-89C headed for Iceland so the 57th FIS could relieve the 82nd FIS that was stationed there with F-94Bs. In turn, the 82nd FIS would give their F-94s to the ANG and obtain F-89Ds, and also rejoin the ADC at Presque Isle. At this time Lt. Colonel Edward Staley replaced "Tex" Hanley as commanding officer.

The 57th FIS staged through Goose Bay, Bluie West 1, and on to Keflavik, usually in flights of four, and met returning flights of F-94s in the process. On November 12 the 57th FIS was officially assigned to the 65th Air Division and MATS at Keflavik.

The 18th FIS had been activated at Minneapolis-St. Paul International Airport, Minnesota, in December 1952 to replace the 109th FIS of the Minnesota ANG that was being relieved from Federal Service after their Korean Conflict activation. Initially they took over the 109th FIS's F-51Ds, but then re-equipped with F-86As in the spring of 1953. This was followed by a short term switch to F-86Fs the following fall.

On January 7, 1954, the 18th FIS became ADC's first F-89D squadron with the receipt of their first example. At this time they were assigned to the 514th ADG under the 31st AD, CADF. As the 18th FIS had already been scheduled for overseas deployment, forecasted for 1955-56, and their transition into Scorpions had been faster than anticipated, their deployment date was revised to September 1954. The last of their assigned twenty-five F-89Ds arrived in July, and on July 26 the relocation of the squadron to Ladd AFB, Fairbanks, Alaska, commenced. On September 1, 1954 the 18th FIS was officially transferred from ADC to the AAC.

The 438th FIS was the next F-89D squadron. Assigned to Kinross AFB, south of Sault Saint Marie, Michigan (Later Kinchloe AFB), the 438th had been activated there with F-94Bs on April 27, 1953, and assigned to the 534th Air Defense Group, CADF.

In the spring of 1954 their F-94s were transferred to the ANG and the first of their assigned twenty-four F-89Ds arrived. At this time their squadron commander was Colonel Thomas Tilley. In June 1957 their number had been reduced to only seven, and the 438th FIS became one of ADC's first F-102 squadrons that summer.

The 497th FIS had been activated at Portland International Airport, Portland, Oregon, on February 18, 1953, and was the last ADC squadron to be assigned F-94As. At this time they were assigned to the 503rd ADG. In the spring of 1954 they began to receive the first of their F-89Ds, and by the end of June they had twenty-four on hand.

On August 18, 1955, as a part of Project Arrow, the 497th FIS designation was moved to Geiger AFB, Washington, and they rejoined their original parent 84th Fighter Group. (At Geiger they replaced in obligation the 520th FIS, a F-86D squadron that was inactivated.)

Effective on this date, August 18, the ex-497th FIS contingent at Portland became redesignated as the 460th FIS, which had been transferred "Less Personnel & Equipment" from McGhee-Tyson AFB, Knoxville, Tennessee, under Project Arrow. They were now assigned to the newly reactivated 337th Fighter Group (Air Defense), of which they had no previous relationship. Colonel George Ceuleers was the new Group commander. In May 1958 the 460th FIS converted to F-102As. Both the 497th and 460th FIS's were under the operational control of the 27th Air Division.

The 337th FIS was activated at Minneapolis-St. Paul IAP, Minnesota, on July 8, 1954, to replace the 18th FIS that was slated for transfer to Alaska. At this time they received twenty-three F-89Ds and were assigned to the 514th ADG.

52-1909, a F-89D assigned to the 76th FIS at Presque Isle AFB. It had been transferred to them from the 75th FIS, and then later modified to a F-89J and assigned to the 179th FIS. via Paul Stevens

A F-89H of the 76th FIS on a cross-country trip to Ethan Allen AFB, Vermont. The winged emblem on the Scorpion's nose carries the assigned aircrews' names and that of its crew chief. -Isham Collection

A F-89J of the 76th FIS at McCoy AFB, which had been renamed from Pinecastle in May 1958, and then closed in July 1974. The 76th had moved to Pinecastle/McCoy AFB in November 1957, and then returned to cooler climates at Westover AFB, New York, in February 1961. -Isham Collection

On August 18, 1955, they were replaced in designation by the 432nd FIS, with their old identification being transferred to a F-86D squadron at Westover AFB, Massachusetts.

On August 5, 1954, the first echelon of the 318th FIS arrived at Presque Isle AFB, Maine, from their NEAC assignment at Thule Air Base, Greenland, as an exchange squadron with the 74th FIS.

Upon their return, their new commanding officer became Major George McCleary, who had been their operations officer in Greenland. At Presque Isle they were assigned directly to the 4711th ADW. On August 20 their first F-89D arrived directly from Northrop, and by the end of September they had twenty-one Scorpions on their roster.

On August 18, 1955, the 318th FIS designation was transferred to McChord AFB, Washington, and the men of the "old" 318th were now designated as the 75th FIS.

The 82nd FIS returned to Presque Isle AFB under a similar move to the 318th FIS. The 82nd FIS had been stationed at Keflavik Air Base, Iceland, and returned to the United States as a replacement for the 57th FIS. While in Iceland they too had been flying F-94s, and they also brought them back with them for further disposition.

Under Major George Beckem, the 82nd FIS was officially transferred from MATS to the ADC and assigned to the 528th ADG, 4711th ADW on October 22. Although they obtained a few new F-89Ds from Northrop, the majority of their Scorpions either came to them from the 57th or 318th FIS's, as both were slated to receive all new aircraft.

In April 1955 Lt. Colonel Walter Hardee was selected as their new squadron commander. Hardee had been the commander of the 26th FIS on Okinawa when the Korean Conflict started.

On Armed Forces Day, May 24, 1955, the 82nd FIS lost their first Scorpion at Williston, Vermont. 1st Lt. Dick Hornbeck and R/O 1st Lt. Robert Leason had an engine failure just after takeoff from Ethan Allen AFB at Burlington, which was followed by a partial loss of power from their other engine. In an attempt to make an emergency landing, they overshot their approach and crashed inverted off the end of the runway. Leason got clear of the wreckage, but Hornbeck was trapped in the aircraft's cockpit and the F-89 had burst into flames. Leason then grabbed a pole and managed to raise the multi-tonned hulk enough so that Hornbeck could crawl to safety. Leason was awarded the Soldier's Medal for his efforts, which at that time was as high an award as the USAF could give him in peacetime.

On August 18, 1955, the 82nd FIS designation was transferred to Travis AFB, California, to replace the 413th FIS, a F-86D squadron at Travis AFB, California, whose designation was being inactivated under Project Arrow. The men of the "old" 82nd FIS thus were redesignated as the 76th FIS.

The 11th FIS had been activated at Duluth International Airport, Duluth, Minnesota, in December 1952 to replace the locally based 179th FIS of the Minnesota ANG that was being returned to State Control after its Korean Conflict Federal activation. Initially the 11th FIS flew F-51Ds, and then F-86Ds.

During the first half of 1955 the 11th FIS converted to F-89Ds, having twenty-eight on hand by the end of June. At this time they were assigned to the 515th Air Defense Group, 31st Air Division. On August 18, 1955, the 515th ADG was inactivated and replaced by the 343rd FIG, with Colonel George Hicks III, commanding. During June 1956 they had twenty-three F-89Ds, but right after that they began conversion to F-102As and by the end of October they had disposed of the last of their Scorpions and were combat ready in the "Deuce."

The 58th FIS had been stationed at Otis AFB, Massachussets, and assigned to the 4707th ADW while flying F-94Cs. In February 1953 they were further assigned to the 564th ADG. Conversion from Starfires to F-89Ds began in early 1955, and by the end of June they had sixteen on hand. On August 18, 1955, Project Arrow took effect, and the 58th FIS rejoined their reactivated and original 33rd Fighter Group. The initial Group Commander was Colonel Fred Hook, who was replaced by Colonel David Tudor in 1956. The 58th FIS was commanded by Lt. Colonel John Delapp. By the end of the year, the number of F-89Ds had increased to twenty-six.

The 33rd FIG, with the 58th FIS flying F-89s and the 60th FIS flying F-94s, was responsible for the air defense of the US's eastern seaboard from the south of Maine to New York. In addition, the 58th FIS was tasked with working with the Lincoln Laboratory, the USAF's contractor through MIT, for the early development of the Data-Link program. An additional program was the exploration of the ACA, Aircraft Controlled Approach. This program utilized radar reflectors that were strategically placed next to Runway 24 at Otis and were tuned to the F-89s radar frequency. This permitted them to be picked up on the Scorpions radar and be differentiated from the ground clutter, "grass," on the Radar Intercept

A pair of 321st FIS F-89Ds over Washington on April 4, 1956. 53-2639 was destroyed on January 21, 1964, when its left engine exploded on the ramp at Des Moines, Iowa, during a ground run-up. At that time it belonged to the 124th FIS. -USAF

Operator's (RIO) scope. With the outline of Cape Cod being very apparent to the RIO, all that had to be done was further align the F-89 with the radar reflectors and at a predetermined point start the penetration, with additional fine tuning corrections being made as the F-89 approached Otis. The crews got to the point where they were as accurate as a GCA or ILS approach, but the system was never approved for operational use.

In the fall of 1956 the F-89Ds were replaced by F-89Hs, with twenty-six being assigned by the end of the year. In the spring of 1957 the F-89Hs were transferred to the 75th FIS at Presque Isle AFB, and replaced by F-89Js, with twenty-eight on board by the end of June. As with other ADC squadrons, the 58th FIS flew to Vincent AFB for rocket training with the Genie missiles. They flew against targets towed by B-57s on the end of a mile-long reel, and were scored by cameras on the Canberra. And, as with the other F-89 squadrons scheduled into Vincent, these training missions had to be flown only during the early morning hours or late at night, as the weight of the F-89s was heavy enough to break through the asphalt taxiways at Vincent during the daytime heat. (Not to mention that the runways were considered to be a couple miles of too short to get the F-89s airborne when it was hot). On August 2, 1959, the 58th FIS was relocated from Otis to Walker AFB, Roswell, New Mexico, with twenty-four Scorpions. They were inactivated at Walker on December 25, 1959, being the second from the last ADC squadron to fly the F-89.

The 63rd FIS was the only squadron of what had originally been the famous WWII 56th Fighter Group, "Zemke's Wolfpack," to fly the F-89 while assigned to the Air Defense Command. When stationed at Wurtsmith AFB, Oscoda, Michigan, the 63rd FIS switched from F-86Ds to F-89Ds in early 1955, and by the end of June they had twenty-seven Scorpions assigned.

While at Wurtsmith, the 63rd FIS was attached to the 4706th Air Defense Wing, which was based at O'Hare IAP, Park Ridge, Illinois. On August 18, 1955, under Project Arrow, the 63rd FIS designation was transferred to O'Hare to replace the 42nd FIS, a F-86D squadron whose designation was thus transferred to Greater Pittsburgh, Pennsylvania. Replacing the 63rd FIS designation at Wurtsmith was the 445th FIS. Also, under Project Arrow the 4706th ADW was inactivated on August 18 and replaced by the newly reactivated 56th Fighter Group at O'Hare.

Back at Presque Isle AFB, the 75th and 76th FISs had both been reactivated on August 18, 1955, under Project Arrow. Both of these squadrons were assigned to the also newly reactivated 23rd Fighter Interceptor Group, which replaced in designation the 528th Air Defense Group. The new 23rd FIG continued under the control of the 4711st ADW, which was commanded by Colonel William Greenwood at this point in time. Lt. Colonel Frank O'Connor was the commander of the 23rd FIG upon reactivation. Lt. Colonel Frank Keller became the Group commander in late October 1955, and he was followed by Colonel Lee McGowan in June 1956; Colonel Orville Kinkade on July 13, 1958; and finally Colonel George McCord in July. The 23rd FIG was inactivated once again on July 30, 1959.

52-1834 came to the 465th FIS from the 4750th Test Squadron at Tyndall AFB when the 465th FIS was activated, and later went to the 132nd FIS at Dow AFB. -via Larry Davis

As the 75th FIS replaced the 318th FIS in designation only, their commanding officer, Major George McCleary, retained his command. Major Luverne Johnson was operations officer.

Flying out of Presque Isle AFB was probably the most hazardous location in the contiguous United States, due to prevailing weather. Also, it was from here that most of the air defense scrambles had the impetuous of being under actual war time conditions, as the tracks of the unknown targets were generated from out of desolate Canada or from over the Atlantic Ocean. Thus the F-89 crews from Presque Isle had the dubious distinction of some of the highest operational F-89 accident rates in ADC's inventory. They had to scramble regardless of the weather, for they just never knew whether it was "for real," or not.

Prior to conversion to F-89Hs the 75th FIS had three F-89Ds destroyed in operational accidents, fortunately without loss of life. However, on December 11, 1958, 1st Lt. David St. Clair and R/O 1st Lt. Roger Sundhal were killed at Presque Isle when they landed a mile and a half short of the runway in their F-89H. Three months later, on March 24, 1959, Lt. Fred Hudson and R/O 1st Lt. Larry Turki also crashed on final approach while returning from a scramble, with Turki being killed.

In April 1959 the 75th FIS F-89Hs started to be transferred to Pennsylvania's 111th FIG at Philadelphia and on May 11 the 75th FIS was relieved of their alert commitment to prepare for a transfer to Dow AFB and conversion to F-101Bs. Lt. Colonel John Bell was their last commanding officer during their Scorpion era.

The 76th FIS replaced the 82nd FIS in designation at Presque Isle and gained their F-89Ds upon activation on August 18, 1955. Lt. Colonel Walter Hardee retained his position as squadron commander.

In March 1956 the 76th FIS obtained twenty-four brand new F-89Ds from Northrop, and turned their worn-down ones over to the 75th FIS, which did not go over all too well! Also,

during the summer of 1956 the USAF originated Project Blue Flame, which transferred higher ranking staff officers back to operational units. Under this, Lt. Colonel Frank Keller replaced Lt. Colonel Hardee. (In many squadrons this was not a happy situation, as when "desk weenies" relieved combat operational pilots, squadron morale among the other pilots suffered through a lack of leadership proficiency.)

On July 17, 1956, the 76th FIS was enroute to Yuma County Airport, Arizona (Later Vincent AFB), for rocket firing practice in their F-89Ds when they had their first operational accident at McConnell AFB, Kansas. After refueling, the second flight of four took off and the number four aircraft in the flight, flown by 2nd Lt. Noah Gregg with R/O 2nd Lt. Harville Hobbs had its left engine catch on fire just after breaking ground. Hobbs ejected at 350 feet while Gregg struggled to get the Scorpion higher. At 700 feet control of the fighter was lost, and Gregg also ejected. Both were uninjured.

The following Friday Lt. Colonel Frank Mattingly and R/O Robert Walz were in the process of making a live rocket attack on a fabric sleeve target towed behind a B-57E. They hit the sleeve's stabilizing bar, and the bar was ingested into their left engine, which exploded. Both ejected okay.

The 76th FIS's last operational loss while stationed at Presque Isle AFB occurred on November 29, 1956, when the F-89 flown by 1st Lts. Charles Holly and R/O Edward Skowron flew into the ground after takeoff. Both were killed.

Major Morris Wilson assumed command of the 76th FIS in 1957 prior to the squadron's move to Pinecastle AFB, Florida. (Later McCoy AFB.) At this time they received some F-89Hs from the 75th FIS, and others directly from Northrop.

On November 9 the 76th FIS departed Presque Isle for Pinecastle. During the summer of 1959 they traded their H model Scorpions in for F-89Js, having twenty-eight on hand by the end of the year. In December 1960 the 76th FIS was programmed for transfer to Westover AFB, Massachussets, and conversion to F-102s. By the end of the year they had only four F-89Js left and were starting F-102 training. On February 1, 1961, they were at Westover and operational in the "Deuce," having been the last continental operational ADC F-89 squadron (except for the later arriving 57 to FIS).

The 321st FIS was activated on August 18, 1955, at Paine AFB, Washington, under Project Arrow. At this time they replaced the 83rd FIS in designation, and received their F-86Ds. The 321st FIS came under direct control of the 326th FIG which had replaced the 529th ADG, also effective August 18, which was commanded by Colonel Ira Wintermute. Wintermute is noted as the first Korean War commander of the 18th Fighter Bomber Group.

Conversion to F-89Ds from Sabres started soon thereafter, and by the end of the year they had twenty-eight available. The 321st FIS was the second ADC squadron selected to receive F-89Hs, and by June 1956 they had thirteen (with thirteen F-89Ds remaining). However, by the end of the year they still had ten Ds, and only fourteen Hs. The following year, by June 1957, the F-89H was already being removed from the USAF inventory, and the 321st FIS had only twelve Hs and had received thirteen F-89Js.

The 321st FIS had twenty-eight F-89Js when they were inactivated on March 1, 1960, and their J models were turned over to the Air National Guard.

The 460th FIS designation was transferred to Portland International Airport, OR from McGhee-Tyson AFB on August 18, 1955 under Project Arrow. At Portland IAP the 460th FIS replaced the 497th FIS, whose designation had been transferred to Geiger AFB, Washington, to replace the 520th FIS.

At Portland, the 460th FIS was assigned to the 337th FIG, which replaced the 503rd ADG under Project Arrow. Colonel George Ceuleers was their commanding officer.

The 460th FIS retained their obtained F-89Ds during their Scorpion era, and by May 1958 they had converted to F-102As.

The 445th FIS had been activated at Geiger AFB, Washington, in March 1953 with F-86Ds, and under Project Arrow their designation was transferred to Wurthsmith AFB, Michigan, to replace the 63rd FIS whose designation had been returned to the 56th Fighter Interceptor Group. The 445th FIS was thus now assigned to the newly reactivated 412th FIG, which was also headquartered at Wurtsmith, under Colonel Ralph Taylor. (The 412th FIG had been the Air Force's first jet fighter group with P-59s and P-80s, and the 445th was one of their original squadrons.) Lt. Colonel Weston Lennox was the 445th FIS squadron commander. He had been a P-47 pilot during WWII and had been shot down over France in 1944.

In March 1956 the 445th FIS received their first two F-89Hs, and they were the first ADC squadron to receive this version of the Scorpion, some two years later than originally scheduled. Further teething problems showed up with the Hs as the 445th attempted to get them operational, as the battery squibs kept blowing when they attempted to get the Falcon missiles ready for combat status. With this resolved, the 445th then earned the ADC's "A" Award, which was given to squadrons that distinguished themselves by an outstanding achievement. Eighteen months later the F-89H was replaced by the F-89J, thus the 445th FIS also had the distinction of flying the F-89H longer than any other ADC squadron.

The 445th did have one slightly humorous incident occur when one of their Scorpions landed with a small fire in the aircraft. As the aircraft slowed on the runway, both crew members evacuated the cockpit by climbing out onto the wing, and then both men pulled their ripcords and jumped the six feet to the ground. The abandoned Scorpion continued off the end of the runway and came to rest without further damage.

In the fall of 1959 the 445th F-89Js were replaced by F-101Bs, with only eight Scorpions remaining by the end of the year. Conversion to VooDoos was completed in early 1960.

The 432nd FIS F-89 era was another Project Arrow transfer. On August 18, 1955, the 432nd FIS designation was relocated from Truax AFB to Minneapolis-St. Paul IAP to replace

Loading a 29th FIS F-89J with a Genie for the 1958 William Tell Rocket Meet, the first competitive meet for the Genie (Although the warhead was inert). The 29th FIS represented the CADF in the Scorpion category. -USAF

the 337th FIS. The 432nd FIS had originally been activated at Truax to replace the 126th FIS of the Wisconsin ANG after their Korean Conflict activation had expired. Of late, they had been flying F-86Ds.

At Minneapolis-St. Paul IAP the "new" 432nd FIS had twenty-two F-89Ds at the end of 1955 and began conversion to F-89Hs in early 1956, possessing twelve F-89Ds and thirteen F-89Hs by the end of June. The 432nd FIS was assigned to the 475th Fighter Interceptor Group under Colonel David Gould, and the 475th FIG had replaced the inactivated 514th ADG under Project Arrow.

On January 2, 1958, the 432nd FIS was inactivated and their entire facility and aircraft were turned over to the 109th FIS of the Minnesota ANG.

The 465th FIS had been inactivated on August 18, 1955, at McChord AFB, Washington, as there was no other unit for them to swap designations with. However, on October 6, 1955, the squadron was reactivated from scratch at Griffiss AFB, New York, to receive F-89Ds as their mission aircraft. Their new commanding officer was Major John Wallace, with Captain William Matthews as operations officer. Both of these men had come from the 27th FIS, as did a majority of the new squadron's personnel.

The 465th FIS received their first Scorpions on February 13, 1956, with nine more arriving in April, and they had a total of fourteen by May. By the end of June they gained thirteen F-89Hs, becoming one of the first squadrons to receive the Falcon equipped aircraft. Also during this period Lt. Colonel Hal Knowles replaced Major Wallace under Project Blue Flame.

On February 8, 1957, the 4727th Air Defense Group was activated at Griffiss AFB with Colonel Frank Keller as commanding officer. At this time the 465th FIS was transferred from the 4711th ADW to the 4727th ADG.

On September 5, 1958, 1st Lt. Thomas Malone and R/O John Doughtry had to bail out of their Scorpion after their left engine exploded during a join-up with a formation of F-94s. The ejections were successful. The reader will note the many ejections from the F-89 after the loss of the left engine. The right engine provided thrust, whereas the left engine also powered the hydraulic flight control systems. If the right engine was lost, only power was lost, but when the left engine quit, control of the aircraft was usually also lost.

The day before Thanksgiving, November 27, 1958, another crew was not as successful. Captain Roy Schellhous and R/O 2nd Lt. John Hartzfeld were up on a practice interception mission against a B-47 when they disappeared from their AC&W controller's radar scope. The wreckage of their F-89 was found the following morning smashed directly into Panther Mountain. No reason for their loss could be determined.

In April 1958 the 465th FIS was declared the top EADF F-89 squadron. This was followed by representing the EADF in the 1958 William Tell World-Wide Weapons Meet at Tyndall AFB, Florida. They won First Place hands-down, scoring 39,500 out of a possible 40,800 points to win in the F-89 category.

On July 1, 1959, the 465th FIS's designation was exchanged with that of the 49th FIS and they became one of ADC's last F-86L squadrons at this time.

The 437th FIS was another Project Arrow transfer which, as far as the squadrons involved were concerned, did not involve a change in equipment. On August 18, 1955, the 437th FIS's designation was transferred from Otis AFB, Massachusetts, to Oxnard AFB, California, where they replaced the 354th FIS in title. (The "old" 354th FIS's designation then went to McGhee-Tyson AFB to become a F-86D squadron.) Lt. Colonel "Sweede" Jenson was their commanding officer at the time of "Arrow," and upon his transfer to Headquarters ADC in the spring of 1956, Lt. Colonel Mulligan became the squadron commander.

At the time of the "Arrow" move both the 354th and 437th FIS's had been flying F-94Cs, so the "new" 437th FIS continued with Starfires until April 1956 when they converted to F-89Ds. The "new" 437th FIS was now assigned to 414th FIG, which had replaced the 533rd ADG at Oxnard, with Colonel Edwin Carey commanding both units. Carey had been a P-40 pilot in China.

The 437th FIS was the only F-89 squadron to actually fire against an intended legitimate target. In August 1956 two of their F-89Ds were scrambled from Oxnard against a U. S. Navy F6F Hellcat drone that had escaped from its radio controller at Point Magu, California.

The Hellcat had been launched as a missile target, but as soon as it broke ground and its landing gear had been retracted, radio control was lost. The aircraft, trimmed for climb, spiraled up to 31,000 feet, and then slowly started to

drift south in large circles towards Los Angeles. While arguments between the USN and the USAF took place as to who would be responsible to bring down the wayward Hellcat, the "what ifs" scenarios created bedlam at the Los Angeles Air Defense Sector.

The Hellcat entered the westerlies, the prevailing off shore winds at its altitude, and then started to drift over Palmdale, Lancaster, and Edwards AFB areas. The two 437th FIS F-89Ds were scrambled and intercepted the F6F, and the F-89 pilots and their ROs discussed their options. The Hughes FCS gave them the choice of firing their rockets in a wings-level attitude under its Phase III method, or under Phase II, firing while both the interceptor and its target were turning.

They selected Phase II, and each F-89 made an interception, got their "splash signal," but their rockets refused to fire. They repeated their Phase II interceptions, and again the rockets refused to fire, and it was later discovered that the system would not work under this configuration, due to a design glitch.

The next option selected was to fire visually. Their F-89Ds had originally been delivered with gunsights, but these had just been removed the month before. It was decided to set the intervalometer to fire twenty-six rocket salvos at a time, which would give each F-89 four opportunities to hit the F6F.

The first Scorpion lined up on the Hellcat and its pilot "Mark 1 eyeballed" the F6F and fired, shotgunning the Hellcat without effect. The second F-89 lined up and fired his rockets, and all went underneath the target. The F-89s lined up again and each readjusted their intervalometers to salvo off their remaining rockets, as by this time the F-89s were starting to run low on fuel. They all missed.

As the Hellcat continued its loose orbit, the fired Mighty Mouse rockets began to fall to earth. One went through an

The 54th FIS at Ellsworth AFB, South Dakota, was one of the short-lived Scorpion squadrons that converted to F-89Js from F-86Ds in the Fall of 1957. They were inactivated in December 1960. Both of the two examples shown here then went to the 103rd FIS to replace their antiquated F-89Hs. -Bill Curry

A 319th FIS F-89J with a 30th Air Division insignia upon its tail parked on the military side of the airfield at O'Hare IAP, Illinois. The 319th, based at Bunker Hill AFB, Indiana, originally fell under the control of the 58th Air Division. -P. D. Stevens via David Menard

engine block of a pickup truck on Highway 395. Another blew a hole in a street in Lancaster. Rockets rained down all over the area, but nothing was hurt but the Air Force's pride. The F6F finally ran out of fuel and crashed in the desert, probably laughing all the way down.

By the end of June 1956 the 437th FIS had twenty-four F-89Ds, but the newer H models were scheduled, and by the end of the year they had eleven D models remaining and twelve H models. The 437th FIS represented the WADF and the 27th Air Division during the 1956 USAF Gunnery and Weapons Meet (Interceptor Phase) at Yuma AFB. The team of Colonel E. F. Carey and Lt. C. E. Lockwood placed Second. The F-89H models continued to be short-lived, and by the end of June 1958 they had been replaced in the 437th FIS by twenty-three F-89Js. By the end of December 1959 the 437th Scorpions in total were in a phase-out, with only nine remaining and F-101Bs beginning to arrive.

The 98th FIS was activated at Dover AFB, Delaware, on March 8, 1956, and they were assigned to the 4709th ADW, which was headquartered at McGuire AFB, New Jersey. By the end of June they had five F-89Ds, and by the end of the year, only thirteen were on their roster.

In early 1957 the F-89Ds were to give way to F-89Hs, but before this program was completed, it was decided to switch the squadron to F-89Js. Thus by the end of June they had two and thirteen examples on hand, respectively. On February 1, 1959, control of the 98th FIS was transferred to the Washington Air Defense Sector and in March they began

conversion to F-101Bs. Their F-89Js would be transferred to another ADC squadron in Arizona.

On April 1, 1957, the Northeast Air Command was inactivated and control of the NEAC assigned squadrons was transferred to the ADC. Included in the return to ADC assignment was the 74th FIS at Thule, the 59th FIS at Goose Bay, and the 61st FIS at Ernest Harmon. All of these squadrons remained attached to the 64th Air Division, which also now came under ADC.

In May 1957 the 29th FIS at Malmstrom AFB, Montana, converted from F-94Cs to F-89Hs, being the only USAF squadron to convert from another type of interceptor directly to the H model Scorpion. At the end of June they had eighteen F-89Hs, but by the end of the year this number had dropped to thirteen, as F-89Js were scheduled for assignment to the 29th FIS.

By June 1958 the 29th FIS was equipped with twenty-six F-89Js and in October they deployed to Tyndall AFB to represent the CADF in the Scorpion category at the First Annual William Tell competition. They placed second, scoring 33,200 out of the possible 40,800 points. In 1959 they again represented CADF with their Scorpions, and placed second once again.

On April 1, 1960, their first F-101B arrived and by June the 29th FIS was considered a VooDoo squadron.

The 54th FIS had been activated at Rapid City AFB, (Later Ellsworth AFB), South Dakota, to replace South Dakota's

175th FIS when they returned to State Control after their Korean Conflict activation. Initially equipped with F-51Ds, and later F-84Gs and F-86Ds, the 54th FIS converted directly into F-89Js in the fall of 1957. They had seven on hand by the end of the year. By June 1958 the 54th FIS had twenty-eight and resumed combat alert.

In 1959 the 54th FIS became the only Scorpion equipped ADC squadron to win the Hughes Achievement Trophy for excellence as an ADC squadron. Unfortunately, this did not prolong their history, for on Christmas Day 1960 the 54th FIS was inactivated.

The 319th FIS at Bunker Hill AFB (Later Grissom AFB), Indiana, converted to F-89Js from F-94Cs in the spring of 1957. The 319th FIS was the only current ADC all-weather squadron with a recent combat history, as they had returned from service in the Far East in November 1955 after knocking down several MiG 15s with their F-94Bs during the Korean War.

By the end of December 1957 the 319th FIS had twenty-six F-89Js and were on their way to becoming one of the sharpest Scorpion squadrons, in both talent and appearance. Their Scorpions all had painted white sidewall tires.

The 319th FIS, under Lt. Colonel Clark Van Deusen, represented the EADF in the 1958 William Tell at Tyndall AFB and came away in First Place in the F-89 category. The top scoring team in that meet was Captain Billy S. Linebaugh and R/O 1st Lt. Donald Price.

On February 2, 1960, the 319th became one of the first ADC F-106 squadrons with the arrival of the Delta Dart.

The 15th FIS at Davis-Monthan AFB, Tuscon, Arizona, was the last squadron to join ADC's inventory with Scorpions. On January 5, 1959, the 15th FIS terminated their alert commitment with F-86L Sabres and commenced conversion to F-89Js. At this time they were under the control of the 34th Air Division at Kirtland AFB, New Mexico, Colonel Richard Kight commanding, and assigned to the CADF.

Lt. Colonel William Reynolds commanded the 15th FIS at the time the first F-89Js arrived from the 98th FIS at Dover AFB for transition training. In a rather exceptional feat, by the end of the first quarter of 1959 97% of the pilots and 100% of the newly arrived R/Os had completed their training. 14% of the pilots and 29% of the R/Os were considered combat qualified. In fairness to the pilots for the lopsided percentages, the pilots had to conduct their transition training from Sabres to Scorpions at Davis-Monthan, while the ROs had the advantage of training with experienced Air National Squadrons in Montana and Minnesota.

On June 3, 1959, Lt. Colonel William McVey relieved Lt. Colonel Reynolds, and Reynolds went to the Air War College. In late fall 1959 the 15th FIS deployed to McDill AFB for Operation Peak-Up and live firing from their F-89s for the first time. In another exceptional action, Lt. John Holaqueen and R/O Collipi fired 100%.

In late winter 1960 many of the 15th FIS F-89Js were flown to Mobile, Alabama, to be turned over to the Alabama Air National Guard, an action that was not completed by the ANG. In April the remaining F-89Js departed for James Connelly AFB and assignment to the Air Training Command, and the 15th FIS became a VooDoo squadron.

Chapter Three: In The Northern Climes

The Cold War defense of Alaska and environs was a complex situation, due to many factors—not the least of which were the great distances involved and the frigid arctic temperatures that had to be contended with.

During World War II the Japanese threat had been concentrated upon Attu and neighboring islands on the far end of the Aleutian Chain, and it was believed that further Japanese attacks would continue eastward along this same string of islands. The United States military forces were finally marshalled, at first for defensive purposes and then for offensive missions, against Japan along this same string of islands. Air bases, sea ports, and army forts were constructed, placed in use, and then largely abandoned as this portion of what was

Captain Ralph Ethridge, 65th FIS. On October 29, 1953, he had to eject from F-89C 50-777 after an engine explosion. His radar observer failed to get out of the aircraft and was killed in the crash. -Roger Lincoln

an unheralded combat theater drifted even further into the backwaters of the war.

In the immediate Post War years the Aleutian Chain did continue to be the focus of attention by the 11th Air Force and the US Navy for the defense of Alaska, as it was felt that any threat to Alaska by the increasingly aggressive Soviets would be via this route. This remained the case until it was discovered that Russia had developed an intercontinental bomber and that they would be able to traverse Alaska via polar routes from undetermined air bases deep within Mother Russia.

In 1946 the Air Force placed their 57th Fighter group on Sheyma, on the far end of the Aleutian Chain for defensive purposes. (The 57th FG actually replaced, in designation, the 343rd Fighter Group which was deactivated on Shemya at this time under a policy of only retaining lower numbered combat units.) Briefly equipped with P-38s, the 57th FG switched to P-51H Mustangs in late summer 1946.

In addition, the 415th Fighter Squadron (All Weather) was transferred from Shaw Field, South Carolina, to Davis Field, on Adak Island on May 19, 1947, with P-61 Black Widows. On September 1, 1947, the 415th FS(AW) was inactivated and replaced in designation by the reactivated 449th Fighter Squadron (All Weather).

The three squadrons of the 57th FG and the 449th FS(AW) represented the total of the Air Force's tactical strength in the Alaskan Theater for an eighteen month period circa 1947/48. In addition, although the 57th FG had a full complement of aircraft, they operated with less than two fully operational squadrons, due to manpower shortages. The 449th FS(AW) had a bare eight P-61 Black Widows assigned, along with a few support aircraft.

In March 1948 the 57th FG was withdrawn from Sheyma to Ft. Richardson and Elmendorf Field at Anchorage, as it was now felt that any threat by Russia from the Chukotskly Peninsula was remote. (And that logistical support of the Group on Sheyma was too difficult if Russia might attack from that direction.)

The situation appeared at this time that any aggressor forces would in all likelihood use the WWII ALSIB Lend-Lease Route in reverse, via the Bering Sea and Nome, Arkansas. To counteract this possible event the 57th FG started using Galena and McGrath Fields as staging bases, along with Marks Field at Nome, for their tactical training missions. At this time the Cold War was just getting started with the communist takeover of Czechoslovakia and the Berlin Airlift situation. Russia's strategic airpower was still believed to be close to nil, but their tactical strength was believed to be high; equipped with United States WWII era Lend-Lease aircraft, if nothing else.

52-1891 was assigned to the 65th FIS in November 1954 to replace their F-89Cs. It was later modified to a J model and served with the 319th FIS, and later on was one of the last Scorpions to serve with the 132nd FIS. -via Paul Stevens

As the Cold War intensified the 449th FS(AW) was withdrawn from Davis Field and reestablished at Ladd Field, Fairbanks. This move took place in March 1949 with the squadron re-equipping with F-82H Twin Mustangs at the same time. In addition, the 57th FG gave up their Mustangs and re-equipped with F-80 Shooting Stars. Although still limited in strength, the Alaskan Air Command, which had replaced the 11th Air Force in designation, now possessed the latest available jet and all-weather fighter types.

In late spring and the early summer of 1951 the 57th, now designated as Fighter-Interceptor Group, converted from F-80s to F-94Bs. Their mission was revised from tactical to air defense.

In August 1952 the 449th, now redesignated as a Fighter-Interceptor Squadron, doubled in size and began to receive F-94As to supplement their Twin Mustangs. They would continue with both types of all-weather fighters until November 1953 when the last operational USAF F-82 was retired.

While all of these changes in aircraft types and roles were taking place, some administrative changes also took place which effected the hierarchy within the parent Alaskan Air Command. On March 15, 1948, the 57th Fighter Wing had been established under the Hobson Wing-Base Plan at Elmendorf Air Force Base, which replaced the previous Air Base Unit, and the 57th FW became the controlling unit for Elmendorf and the 57th FG. Colonel Thomas Mosley was the first of five 57th FW commanding officers during this period. An Air Force reorganization on January 20, 1950, redesignated the 57th FW, FG and FSs as FIW, FIG and FISs, respectively. On January 1, 1951, the 57th FIW was inactivated and replaced in designation by the newly created 10th Air Division. Colonel James Andrew being the last 57th FIW commander, and the first for the 10th AD.

On April 13, 1953, the 57th FIG itself was inactivated and its three fighter-interceptor squadrons, the 64th, 65th, and 66th FISs were placed under the direct control of the 10th AD. This move did away with a full level of administrative control, which was felt to have been redundant.

At Ladd AFB the 449th FIS had previously been under the direct supervision of the 5001st Composite Wing, which was the controlling agency for Ladd. On April 8, 1953, the 5001st CW was inactivated and replaced by the newly activated 11th Air Division.

With this background in mind, prior to the arrival of the F-89 in Alaska we can see that the USAF had four all-weather squadrons based in Alaska under the control of two autono-

A 64th FIS F-89D. The 64th's insignia, although in use for decades, was not officially approved until July 1956. Perhaps it was the most appropriate insignia of any of the Scorpion squadrons, as it was that of a scorpion. -USAF

mous Air Divisions. The USAF's tactical and strategic strength was minimal, with a few selected Tactical and Strategic Air Command squadrons rotating through Ladd and the old Mile 26 Air Base (renamed Eielson AFB on January 13, 1948) southeast of Fairbanks.

The jurisdictional breakdown between the 10th and 11th Air Divisions was roughly on a direct east-west line running from Romanzof on Alaska's western coast to Clear, to just south of Eielson AFB and to the Canadian boarder. The 10th AD was responsible for everything south of this line, including the now isolated Sheyma AFB. (The US Navy had assumed responsibility for the remainder of the Aleutian Chain.) The 11th AD controlled everything to the north of this line.

In 1946 the Army-Navy Hoge Board had recommended that thirty-seven radar sites should be established in Alaska to provide for early warning in the event of intruders in the area. Yet by 1949, due to budget cutbacks, little had been done and the recommendation was reduced to just ten sites, of which only three of the old WWII sites were still in continuous operation. The final locations for the remaining seven sites were not even made until the spring of 1950.

Two more site locations were selected in 1951 and construction of the previous seven selected sites finally got underway at this time. It would take until the spring of 1954 to get these sites in operation, at a cost of $46 million. Six more sites would be added, but it would not be until July 1958 before they would become operational.

The Alaskan portion of the aforementioned DEW Line commenced in 1953 with the main location located on Baxter Island. This line stretched from Cape Lisburne to Baffin Island, Canada. Eventually Alaska's DEW Line consisted of six main sites, twenty auxiliary and twenty-eight intermediate radar stations. In 1957 the entire Line was declared opera-

tional, but it had been decided in January to supplement the DEW Line with extensions in Greenland, the Alaskan Peninsula, and the eastern portion of the Aleutian Islands. Of this, the Alaskan Air Command's portion did not become operational until April 1959.

By this time the number of the fighter-interceptor squadrons in Alaska was already being reduced, as it was felt that the threat was no longer via inter-continental bombers, but by ballistic missiles.

The 65th Fighter Interceptor Squadron, based at Elmendorf AFB, was the first Alaskan Air Command recipient of the Scorpion. The first three of their F-89Cs arrived on September 6, 1953, to begin replacement of their F-94Bs. With the exception of these first three examples, half of their remaining complement of aircraft had been transferred from the 433rd FIS at Truax, while the remainder came from the 3625th Pilot Training Squadron at Tyndall AFB, Florida. The first of these already weary Scorpions was lost on October 29 after an engine failure near Elmendorf.

In November 1954 the 65th FIS F-89Cs gave way to new rocket equipped F-89Ds directly from Northrop. One of these being lost at Naknek (later renamed King Salmon Air Force Station), which the 65th FIS used as a forward staging base for interceptor operations in January 1955.

Naknek/King Salmon AFS, in itself is worthy of note: During WWII it had been the most southwestward forward operating base on the North American continent. Served by a Low Frequency Radio Range, and later a Visual Omni Range, VOR, the airbase was located just inside Kvichak Bay, which was inside of Bristol Bay and the Bering Sea. Fog, ice fog, low ceilings and heavy precipitation were the norm. Coupled with no overrun on the approach end of the instrument runway and obstructions that were unmarked on the Instrument Approach Plate to begin with, it was "one hairy place" to operate all-weather fighters from.

Armed and ready to be scrambled against a target. Note the "hot" painted inside each rocket pod to indicate the aircraft's status to ground personnel. -Isham Collection

The 65th FIS won the July 1956 Alaska Air Command Rocketry Meet as a cumulative effort with the 10th AD and narrowly beat out the 11th AD's 449th FIS. 1st Lt. David Riley and RO 1st Lt. Max Ross fired 5800 out of 6000 points and obtained perfect scores in one event, which brought them congratulations from Northrop. They then represented the Alaskan Air Command during the October 1956 Air Defense Command Rocketry Meet at Vincent AFB, Arizona. Although the 65th FIS finished in a tie for seventh place in the meet, the team of 10th AD deputy commander Colonel Donald Graham and his radar observer 1st Lt. Billy Thompson won the High Aircrew Trophy.

On November 1, 1957, the 65th FIS was assigned to Richards-Gebaur AFB, Missouri (previously Grandview AFB), "Without Personnel and Equipment," WOPE. The squadron was inactivated on January 8, 1958, without being remanned or re-equipped.

In June 1954 both the 64th and 66th Fighter Interceptor Squadrons sent their tired F-94Bs to the "Lower 48" where they went to either the 433rd FIS on temporary assignment, or to Air National Guard FISs, and they received brand new F-89Ds in exchange. The 64th FIS lost three of these Scorpions, one in a solo accident, and two via a mid-air collision.

On August 15, 1957, the 64th FIS was transferred to McChord AFB, Washington, as a part of the programmed reduction of Scorpions in Alaska, as by now the threat was believed to be more from ballistic missiles than intercontinental bombers and the AAC was commencing their draw-down of fighter squadrons. The 64th FIS re-equipped with F-102s at McChord.

As in the case of the 65th FIS, the 66th FIS's designation was transferred to the Air Defense Command on December 1, 1957, "Without Personnel and Equipment." The 66th FIS was inactivated at Oxnard AFB, California, on January 8, 1958.

51-11393 of the 18th FIS "Blue Foxes" at Ladd AFB in May 1957. -A/2c Menard

The three 10th Air Division F-89 squadrons at Elmendorf AFB were replaced by two F-102 squadrons, the 31st and 317th FIS's.

Assigned to the 11th Air Division at Ladd AFB, the 433rd FIS "Satan's Angels," arrived at Ladd on July 14, 1954, from Truax AFB with their F-89Cs.

Commencing in September 1955 the 433rd started to re-equip with F-89Ds, with most of their old C models being transferred to Michigan's ANG squadrons.

On November 1, 1957, the 433rd FIS's designation was transferred to Minot AFB, Montana, "Less Personnel and Equipment" with the intention of rebuilding the squadron with new personnel and F-89Js, but instead the 433rd FIS was inactivated on January 8, 1958.

The 18th FIS "Blue Foxes," led by Major John "Buck" Rogers, arrived at Ladd from Minneapolis-St. Paul two weeks behind the 433rd FIS, on July 26, 1954, and they brought the first F-89Ds to Alaska. Although the 18th FIS lost two Scorpions while at Ladd, they did establish a new record for F-89 operations. By late June 1957 one of their Scorpions, 52-1858, had been flown over 1000 hours without requiring any major depot maintenance. In the three year period this particular Scorpion had been serviced by no less than seven crew chiefs.

On August 15, 1955, the AAC started their second annual gunnery and rocketry competition. The 1954 meet featured F-94Bs and F-89Cs with standard armament, while the 1955 meet was all F-89Ds. By August 19 there was a four-way tie taking place between the 18th, 449th, 64th, and 66th FISs. Adverse weather held up the completion of the meet until August 29 and by then the 18th FIS easily placed first with 1st Lts. William Evans and Ben Hoskins being the "top guns," albeit with rockets. The 18th FIS finished the meet with 6,600 points and they and the 11th AD's second place finisher, the 449th FIS, sent their teams to Vincent AFB, Arizona, in October to represent the 10th and 11th ADs in the 1955 ADC Rocketry meet. Although the team of Captains Jack Gillette and RO Samuel Miller drew first blood, the Alaskan teams finished 6,800 points behind the wining F-94C crew.

The ubiquitous firebottle and F-89D 54-186 of the 433rd FIS at Ladd AFB, Fairbanks, Arkansas. The temperature at the time this photograph was taken was -45 degrees. -A/2c Menard

A pair of 449th FIS Scorpions on patrol bearing unusual markings on their F-89s Most had their squadron insignia on both sides of the vertical stabilizer, but these include their Air Division. 53-2675 later went to the 29th FIS at Great Falls AFB and on February 5, 1959 it was flown into the ground and its crew was killed. -Norm Taylor Collection

On August 20, 1957, the 18th FIS was transferred back to the ADC from the AAC and was assigned to Wurtsmith AFB, to be re-equipped with F-102s shortly thereafter.

Although the 449th FIS was the first of AAC's all-weather squadrons, they were the last of the six Scorpion squadrons in Alaska. The finally replaced their obsolescent F-94Bs with F-89Ds under Project AAC 4F 281 in October 1954. The 449th FIS, under Colonel Joseph Marsiglia, shared the huge old Hanger One at Ladd with the 18th FIS.

The 449th FIS lost four F-89Ds while operating from Ladd and their satellite airfield at Galena. They were flying in some of the worst possible weather conditions in Alaska—in addition to snow and ice fog, the Fairbanks environs included some of the coldest winter temperatures recorded. Winter temperatures often reached fifty degrees below Zero, which caused severe cold soak of the airframes and congealing of oil and hydraulic fluids. (The Air Police guard dogs were brought in out of the weather when the temperature reached minus forty degrees, but the ground crews had to endure another ten degree drop before they could seek shelter. Outside maintenance on the aircraft was difficult at best.) Atmospheric disturbances caused the "swing" of the Ladd Radio Range legs, which made navigation in instrument conditions hazardous. Both Ladd and Galena had rivers crossing the approach course at each end of their runways, which created hazards for under or overshoots on approaches, along with heavy migratory waterfowl in the Spring and Fall seasons.

To improve operating conditions an eight stall alert barn was constructed at Ladd and a four stall barn at Galena. These had doors on either end of the stalls that opened simultaneously, which permitted an F-89 being scrambled to be started and placed in afterburner in the barns before even taking the short taxi strips to the runway. The 449th established a record scramble time of two minutes, twenty-eight seconds from the time the scramble horn went off to airborne while launching from one of these barns with a F-89.

In the summer of 1957 the 449th FIS was informed that they were to receive F-102s, but instead they received F-89Js. Some of these were newly modified Ds by Northrop, while others were changed to the J configuration "in the field" via modification kits airlifted in from California.

In January 1960 the Air Force decided to replace the 449th FIS Scorpions with F-104As and a phaseout of the F-89J

A F-89H of the 75th FIS. The 75th inherited all of their H model Scorpions from the 58th FIS when the 58th converted to F-89Js. -USAF

51-5767 of the "Black Knights," the 57th FIS. The 57th became one of the largest single users of the F-89, having no less than 45 aircraft pass through their inventory at one time or another. 51-5767 later went to the 186th FIS at Great Falls, Montana, where it became known as "Conrad." -USAF

"My Mommie III" on liftoff from Thule with flaps at thirty degrees and the blow-in doors open to suck in more air. -via M. Bacon

began, with the last one departing Ladd on July 31, 1960. By this date two more decisions had been made, the first to bring in F-101Bs, and then to inactivate the squadron instead, which took place in August.

NEAC

On the opposite end of the continent and in the Atlantic Ocean areas, the USAF replaced F-94 squadrons in Newfoundland, Greenland, and Iceland with F-89 squadrons. Exactly why these squadrons were exchanged instead of re-equipping the existing squadrons with the newer aircraft cannot be determined. Presumably the USAF wanted ground and aircrews already experienced in the newer type of aircraft in the hostile weather environment, instead of attempting to conduct transition training in adverse climactic conditions.

The controlling command for Newfoundland and Greenland was the Northeast Air Command, NEAC, whose antecedents stemmed from the activation of the Newfoundland Base Command, which had been activated on January

February 1956 and the 57th FIS is receiving their brand new F-89Ds from the last block before F-89H production took over the line. -USAF

15, 1941. The right to build and operate military bases in Newfoundland had been granted to the United States in 1940 in an agreement between the US and Great Britain, as Newfoundland at that time had been a Crown Colony. A similar agreement between the US and Denmark at the same time gave the US the right to become an emergency protectorate of Greenland and gave the US similar construction rights.

During WWII the Newfoundland Base Command, NBC, had been subordinate to the Eastern Defense Command. On January 1, 1946, control of the NBC was transferred to the Atlantic Division, Air Transport Command. As a result of a close election conducted in Newfoundland in 1949, the area separated ties with Great Britain and aligned with Canada to become Canada's 10th Providence on April 1, 1949. Effective October 1, 1950, control of NBC was transferred from what had since become the Military Air Transport Service, MATS, to the newly created Northeast Air Command.

This newly created command was Headquartered at Pepperrell Air Force Base, St. John's, Newfoundland. At inception, five other air bases were under the Command's control: Ernest Harmon Air Base at Stephenville; McAndrew Air Base at Argentia; Goose Air Base, Labrador (Actually a dependency of Newfoundland); Narsarssuak, "Bluie West-One," and Sondrestrom, "Bluie West-Eight," Greenland. Thule Air Base, Greenland, would open in 1952 and in 1955 McAndrew Air Base was turned over to the U.S. Navy.

Additional subordinate bases that had been built in the area during the course of WWII and had been turned over to the Canadian government at the end of the war either were borrowed back or were shared with Canadian forces during NEAC's, and later, ADC's existence. Primarily these were used as AC&W or Airways and Air Communications Service, AACS, sites. Goose Air Base at Goose Bay, Labrador, was the major "shared" air base with the Royal Canadian Air Force and the USAF portion of the base fell under the control of MATS.

Another brand new F-89D-75 with the long range ferry tanks installed is prepared for its transfer to Iceland and assignment to the 57th FIS. The MATS insignia on its nose is unusual even though MATS was its parent assignment. W. J. Balogh, Sr.

At Keflavik International Airport, Iceland, a joint use air base under the control of MATS was shared with the Icelandic Government. This base had been in heavy operation since the early days of WWII and had been the home field for the first Army Air Corps fighter pilot to destroy a German aircraft during that conflict. A continuation agreement signed in May 1951 established the Iceland Air Defense Force, which thus came under the control of MATS and their subordinate 52nd Air Division. (The 52nd AD designation was later transferred to Spain and was replaced by the 65th AD.)

Each of these remote air fields had their own characteristics, all of them adverse to major degrees due to the weather. Thule was the USAF's most northern air base and its first permanent location north of the Arctic Circle. It was known

1959 and once again configured for a ferry flight, this time back to the United States from Iceland, 54-231 of the 57th FIS. At this time the 57th partially converted to J models, retaining some D models, and those were disposed of at Keflavik when they were replaced by F-102s. -Havelarr via Olmsted

for its cold weather, although it did have less snow and fog than the other locations. It was also known for having a woman behind every tree. (Actually it did have one of each for a period, both imported!) Iceland was volcanic in origin and noted for being bombarded by the North Atlantic's variable weather. Although more moderate in temperature than the other locations, it had rapidly changing weather conditions that could trap an unwary pilot with no alternate air fields available. Although there were plenty of exceptionally good looking women in Iceland, fraternization was discouraged. The USAF's presence on Iceland was based upon its political and treaty needs to be there, not upon the native's desire for them. Newfoundland and Labrador and were considered as remote or semi-remote locations and were established as the jumping off sites for the WWII ferry routes for aircraft destined for Europe. Installations remained antiquated, and although the sportsman could find hunting and fishing available, all others suffered due to the desolation. Once again cold, along with heavy snows and fog, made living and working conditions difficult.

The first of the F-94 squadrons to be replaced by a F-89 squadron was the 318th FIS at Thule Air Base, Greenland. The 318th had gone to Thule on July 1, 1953, to replace a detachment of 59th FIS F-94s that had been stationed there on temporary duty when the air base opened for limited operations in September 1952. On August 4 the 74th FIS departed Presque Isle AFB, Maine, with squadron commander Major Richard Crutcher leading. After staging through Goose Bay, Bluie West 1, and Bluie West 8, with their F-89Cs Major Crutcher landed at Thule on August 9, becoming the first F-89 pilot to land north of the Arctic Circle.

On August 10 the 74th FIS, now assigned to the 64th Air Division, NEAC, took over the air defense alert duties at Thule, but it was not until August 25 that the last of their F-89Cs and crews arrived from Maine. In the meantime, the 318th FIS

Into the drink! This 61st FIS Scorpion came to grief on November 20, 1956, after an engine failure on takeoff. The pilot managed to bring it back around for an attempt at an emergency landing, but he was a bit too heavy with fuel and landed too fast, and could not get her stopped on the runway. -via Phillip Huston

moved into their vacated quarters at Presque Isle and turned their F-94s over to the depot, to convert to F-89Ds.

On August 15, 1955 the 74th FIS began transferring their F-89Cs to the Michigan ANG and received F-89Ds. On April 1, 1957, the parent Northeast Air Command was inactivated and the 74th FIS returned to the control of the Air Defense Command, but remained under the direction of the 64th Air Division. On June 25, 1958, the 74th FIS was inactivated at Thule.

In August 1954 the 57th FIS at Presque Isle received two dozen F-89Ds from Northrop and things were looking quite modern, but it was not to be, for as soon as the acceptance checks were accomplished these Scorpions were transferred to the 82nd FIS, and the 57th FIS continued with the older C models, remaining equipped with them when their own alert notice of an impending transfer to Iceland arrived.

Lt. Colonel Edward Staley became the commander of the 57th FIS just prior to their move to Keflavik Air base on November 12, 1954, to replace the 82nd FIS. (While not actually assigned to NEAC, this portion is included here for continuities sake.) The 82nd, and then the 57th FISs were assigned to the 65th Air Division, which was subservient to the Military Air Transport Service, MATS. Along with their forerunners, the 192nd and 435th Fighter Squadrons, while stationed in Iceland, these were the only fighter squadrons to be assigned to MATS during the Post War years.

On October 22, 1954, the 82nd FIS started their transfer to Presque Isle with their F-94Bs and their first contingent got as far as Narsarssuak Air Base, Greenland, before the weather held them up. At Narsarssuak Air Base they met the first group of 57th FIS F-89Cs that were headed the other way, a problem that also affected the second batches of both squadrons aircraft. Finally, on November 10 the Scorpions made it to Keflavik and the last of the 82nd FIS F-94Bs departed. The

82nd FIS would turn their F-94s over to the depot on their return and re-equip with F-89Ds that had arrived to equip the 57th FIS!

In August 1955 the 57th FIS finally obtained F-89Ds of their own, with their C models being transferred to the Michigan and Montana ANG.

The 57th FIS, being the sole representative of the Iceland Defense Force, was in a position of not having to compete with other squadrons to see who would go to ADC's annual gunnery and rocket meet at Vincent AFB, Arizona. In 1955 the 57th FIS placed Seventh, and in 1956 they came in Sixth.

On July 1, 1962, the 57th FIS, now known simply as the "Black Knights," was transferred from the control of MATS back to the Air Defense Command, which once again returned the Scorpion to ADC's inventory for a short period. But two and a half months later the 57th FIS switched to F-102As. These last twelve ADC Scorpions came to an inglorious end, as some were buried in volcanic ash while others were relegated to the fire department at Keflavik and were burned in training exercises.

In Newfoundland the 64th Air Division was the operational institution for NEAC. Also based at Pepperrell Air Base, the 64th AD controlled the operations of the 59th FIS at Goose Bay, the 74th FIS at Thule, and the 61st FIS at Ernest Harmon Air Force Base, Newfoundland. (Ernest Harmon was one of the few Air Force Bases that was not located on United States soil. Due to political concession, almost all air bases located on foreign soil are know as simply "Air Base"(s), while those on US soil are "Air Force Base"(s).

In both 1955 and 1956 the 64th AD pulled what was considered skullduggery by all of the other F-89 fighter-interceptor squadrons when it came to competing in the ADC rocket team competitions. It was ADC's policy that each Air Defense Force would have a fly-off between their assigned squadrons

52-1954 was no stranger to the cold. After serving with the 449th FIS at Ladd AFB as a D model, she was upgraded to a J and assigned to the 59th FIS, and later went to Vermont's 134th. -Halley via Doug Barbier

52-1950 was originally assigned to the 59th FIS under Project NEA-4F-317. In 1959 the 59th was commanded by Leonard Koehler with Patrick Parlavecchia as Operations Officer. -Isham Collection

"Kick the tires and light the fires." 52-1954 goes "gate" (afterburner) at Goose Bay AB. The blow-in doors are open to draw in more air to the engines, and this J model has been modified with the runway arrestor hook. -Isham Collection

to see which squadron would represent the respective ADFs at the rocket meets, yet the 64th AD made up their own composite team from their three assigned squadrons instead. This was considered grossly unfair by the other participants.

In 1955 the 64th AD placed Third with 9,000 points. On the second day of the 1956 meet, Colonel Carroll McColpin, commander of the 64th AD, with 1st Lt. Kenneth Watson as his RO, racked up a perfect score to tie the WADF's 437th FIS. A final tally on the last day of the Meet found the 64th AD's team in Third Place once again, with 9,600 points. (The Meet was won by the 94th FIS flying F-86Ds, while the 437th FIS came in second.)

The 61st FIS had been detached from its original parent fighter group, the famed 56th Fighter Group, "Zemke's Wolfpack" on July 10, 1953, and assigned to Ernest Harmon and the 64th AD with F-94Bs. In December 1953 they began receiving F-89Cs in a slow conversion to that model that took until the end of February 1954 to be completed. They lost one of these C models in an accident on March 5, 1954, and another on September 27. The majority of their old F-94Bs were transferred to the 59th FIS.

In late Spring 1955 the 61st FIS converted to F-89Ds. On April 1, 1957, NEAC was inactivated and control of the 61st FIS transferred to the ADC. At this time the 64th AD was also inactivated and the squadron was assigned to the replacement 4731st Air Defense Group. The 61st FIS had twenty-one F-89Ds in their inventory at this time. On October 17, 1957, the 61st FIS was transferred "Without Personnel and Equipment" to Truax AFB, Wisconsin, with eventual conversion to F-102As when the squadron was remanned.

On September 11, 1952, an advanced detachment of the 59th FIS commenced TDY operations at Thule Air Base with F-94s, and on October 28, 1952, the remainder of the squadron relocated from Otis AFB, Massachussets, to Goose Bay. They were the first fighter squadron to be assigned to NEAC, and the first to be based in a Canadian Province. On July 1, 1953, their detachment at Thule was relieved by the 318th FIS and they rejoined the remainder of the squadron at Goose Bay.

Also assigned to the 64th AD, the 59th FIS was the last of the overseas based F-94 squadrons, not removing their last one from short term storage until 1956. In the meantime, the 59th FIS had commenced receiving F-89Ds in December 1954 under Project NEA 4F 317, and they had twenty-five F-89Ds on hand by the end of January 1955.

When NEAC was inactivated on April 1, 1957, the 59th FIS was also assigned to the ADC and attached to the newly activated 4732nd Air Defense Group at Goose Bay. At this time they had twenty F-89Ds, but by the end of 1957 they had converted to F-89Js, with twenty-nine on hand.

This number of aircraft was reduced by transfer and attrition to twenty-two by the end of June 1959. In February 1960 the 59th FIS switched to F-102As.

Chapter Four: The Air National Guard

Prior to the Korean Conflict, the Air National Guard, ANG, was regarded by many as little more than a federally funded flying club for an elite few citizen soldiers. This, of course, was hardly true, but the political perception was there, along with some civilian elements holding the same thoughts.

For the most part, the early ANG did suffer through a hand-me-down complex, however. All of their early equipment was obsolete: Mustangs, Thunderbolts, Invaders, and miscellaneous transport types made up their flying inventory, and although the majority of these aircraft had not seen actual combat in World War II and were "low time" airframes, they remained as remnants of an earlier era. Finally, in 1949, six ANG squadrons did enter the jet age through receiving brand new, off the production line F-80s that were contracted for by the USAF especially for the ANG. The remainder of the ANG squadrons continued to fly the aged aircraft.

Although some funding did come to the National Guard Bureau for the construction of new and permanent ANG facilities at their civilian airport sites, other funding shortfalls continued to manifest themselves. It was not an uncommon sight to see ANG ground crews working upon their aircraft in partial or full civilian dress, nor was it uncommon for ANG pilots to fly training missions with civilian clothing under their flying suits, as neither officers or enlisted men had a complete set of issued uniforms. Hence the "The Raggity Assed Militia" sobriquet often laid upon the ANG folks.

The Korean Conflict changed all of this, as almost all of the ANG squadrons were recalled into Federal Service, with several of these units seeing combat in Korea, where many of their men paid the highest price while fighting a war that the politicians still have not garnered the courage to call an actual war. Again, in those units that did not go to Korea, some did go to Europe to defend NATO's interest, and many others gave their lives in the process.

The majority of the activated ANG squadrons remained in the United States to serve as training cadre for officers and men who would eventually see service in full-time USAF units. In this, which actually was a dual role, as the activated squadrons also had various other roles, tactical, reconnaissance or air defense, the supreme sacrifice was again paid by many squadron personnel. There was not a single activated ANG squadron that did not lose one or more of their men while on active duty with the USAF during the "Forgotten War."

As these ANG squadrons were called into Federal Service for a period not to exceed twenty-one months, as man-

dated under Federal Law, most returned to their home state on October 31, 1952, as this date marked the end of their recall period. Only about one half of the men that had been recalled returned to their ANG squadrons. Many of the WWII veterans, after having their civilian careers disrupted, elected to add the twenty-one months to their previous four or so years and continued in the USAF to make a new career out of it. Others took the opportunity to accept a discharge and avoid any further contact with the military.

For those that returned to the ANG, they found little initial improvement in their equipment. All of their previous aircraft had been returned to the USAF for service during the conflict, and these were either lost to attrition or worn out. Initially, almost all of them were replaced by a later version of the Mustang, the F-51H, which had been in storage. However, in 1953, some of the squadrons began receiving F-86A and E Sabres, F-80s, and F-84Es that had seen service in Korea, Europe, or the Air Training Command. Brand new F-84F Thunderstreaks were slated for some units, commencing in 1954.

These assignments depended upon the squadron's initial commitment: either air defense, or tactical. However, in the case of an ANG unit having a primary tactical commitment, all were given a secondary air defense commitment for a period encompassing 1954-1957.

In the spring of 1953 the USAF decided to re-equip several of the ANG squadrons assigned an Air Defense Com-

One of the early F-89Ds assigned to the 176th FIS at Truax AFB, Wisconsin. It appears exceptionally sleek in this view, in contrast to the Scorpion's usual general bulky appearance. -Wisconsin ANG photo

OPPOSITE: 51-11332 of the 176th FIS. Note that the standard ANG markings had been revised to that of Air Guard, which occurred circa 1956. -A/2c Menard

53-2646 of the 176th FIS. The sign on the wheel warns that the Scorpion is US government property and for people to keep off of it. This F-89 later went to the Florence Air and Missile Museum, Florence, South Carolina. -Merle Olmsted

The same F-89B, 49-2471, assigned to the 126th FIS on a visit to Detroit Wayne-Major Airport, Michigan, in July 1955. The F-86D belonged to the 325th FIS. The size comparison of the two interceptors is interesting in that the designers had the same mission requirement to fulfill but took an entirely different approach in how to accomplish it, which resulted in such dissimilar aircraft being operational during the same era. -R. Volker via Esposito

mand commitment with all-weather interceptors to bolster their own air defense posture. Initially these would be F-94s that were being replaced in the USAF's inventory by F-86Ds and F-89s. Then, in mid-fall 1954, Scorpions would be available to the Guard, to be followed by F-86s when the future F-102 would be available as a first-line interceptor.

The first F-94s went to squadrons of the New York ANG in June 1953. The first F-89s would go to the ANG in September 1954.

As the 176th FIS at Truax AFB, Wisconsin, had been one of the first F-89 squadrons during their stint with the regular air force during the Korean emergency, they were an obvious choice for re-equipment with the Scorpion when the USAF attempted to modernize the Air National Guard. Thus the 176th FIS became the first ANG squadron to receive F-89s, obtaining their first on September 1, 1954, under Project ADC 2F-11. These were F-89Bs that had been rebuilt by Northrop after having been returned to them for rework from the 84th FIS. By the end of October they would have a complement of thirteen. As with their previous period with the Scorpion, Major Oliver Ryerson was the squadron commander.

The Scorpions replaced a mixed bag of F-51Hs and F-86As, as the Sabres had started to arrive the previous January, but not in a sufficient number to become operational

49-2471, a revamped B model, of the 126th FIS with the F-80s that they replaced in 1955 in the background. -via A/2c Menard

with them, and the last Mustang did not leave until after the F-89s had arrived.

The 176th FIS lost their first F-89B on November 14, 1954, in an accident, with the Scorpion being a write-off.

A major problem facing the 176th FIS, as with all other F-89 and F-94 ANG squadrons, was the lack of available radar observers, as none had been previously required for their aircraft. Fortunately, in the case of the 176th, Truax was a major ADC F-89 base, and they were able to draw some R/Os from these squadrons as these men finished their USAF obligations.

In 1956 Lt. Colonel Thomas Moffatt replaced (now) Lt. Colonel Ryerson as squadron commander, with Ryerson assuming command of Wisconsin's 128th Air Defense Wing.

In July 1957 the F-89Bs and the Cs that had come along in the intervening years were replaced by F-89Ds. The majority of the F-89Cs went to Michigan ANG squadrons, while the B models went to Idaho's 190th FIS. The F-89D meant retraining with rockets, instead of cannons.

In 1958 the 115th Fighter Interceptor Group was activated at Truax with (then) Major Francis Middleton assuming command of the 176th FIS and (now) Colonel Moffatt becoming the commander of the new fighter group. The 176th FIS also suffered its first fatal accident with the Scorpion in 1958 when 1st Lt. Duane Piestorff was killed in an accident at Tinker AFB, Oklahoma.

In 1959 the F-89D gave way to the F-89H for a short period, and in January 1960 the H model was replaced by the F-89J. As Truax AFB was a major USAF installation at the time, the 176th FIS did not have the problems with the care and feeding of the nuclear Genie that their Milwaukee

52-2135 had an interesting history, being a part of NEAC's 1956 rocket team while assigned to the 59th FIS. Later with the 465th FIS it was involved in a mid-air collision with another F-89, but both survived the incident. The 126th FIS originated the vertical stabilizer paint scheme, which was continued by the 124th FIS when Iowa obtained the assets of the 126th from Wisconsin. -Iowa ANG photo via Doug Olson

53-2658 as assigned to the 126th FIS. Note the two barbed barrier hooks and the profile of the engine exhaust deflectors. Northrop spent countless man-hours in development of these deflectors in attempts to control the negative aspects of the engines blasts. -Esposito

counterparts did, and the 176th continued with this version of the Scorpion until F-102s began to arrive in May 1966.

The 176th FIS lost its last F-89 pilot on June 15, 1965, when Captain David Holmberg attempted to abort his take-off. His F-89J engaged the crash barrier satisfactorily, but at too high a speed, and exploded on the overrun before he could evacuate the cockpit.

Until the 115th Fighter Interceptor Wing was activated at Truax, Wisconsin's 128th FIW had been the parent unit for both the 176th and 126th FISs, with the 126th FIS being based at Milwaukee's General Billy Mitchell Field. Colonel Paul Fotjik had assumed command of the 128th FIW upon his return from combat in Korea and the return of the 128th FIW's designation to State Control after the Korean Emergency. In 1955 Fotjik returned to active duty with the USAF, and Colonel Seymour Levenson became the commander of the 128th FIW until its inactivation on April 10, 1958.

When the 128th FIW was inactivated, the 128th Fighter Interceptor Group had to be reorganized, as they had the

53-2536, an F-89D delivered to the 126th FIS as a replacement for their cannon-armed earlier models. Just your basic "Plain Jane" scheme. -Esposito

responsibility for the actual flying unit, the 126th FIS, whereas the FIW had been primarily administrative in function. On April 10, 1958, Lt. Colonel Thomas Bailey was named commander of the reorganized Group.

When the 126th FIS was returned to State Control on October 31, 1952, they obtained first F-51Ds, and then F-86As, in August 1953. On September 25, 1954, their first F-89Bs arrived at Mitchell Field. As in the case of the 176th FIS, these Scorpions were also ex-78th FIG aircraft that had been refurbished by Northrop. Major Paul Dowd was their commanding officer at this time.

The F-89Bs were soon replaced by F-89Cs, with the B models either going to the Idaho ANG or being assigned to Air Training Command functions. In 1957 the C models were replaced by F-89Ds, with the C models going to the Montana ANG. In August 1959 Colonel Levenson was killed in the crash of a F-89D at Milwaukee.

In January 1960 the 126th FIS converted to F-89Js and the 128th FIG was again expanded to Wing size with the reactivation of the 128th FIW. The new Wing also now included the 148th FIG at Duluth, Minnesota, and the 119th FIG at Fargo, North Dakota.

The nuclear equipped F-89J created storage and security problems at Mitchell that could not be overcome, so the 126th FIS was reorganized and became redesignated as an aerial refueling squadron with KC-97s. Their Scorpions were transferred to the 124th FIS at Des Moines, Iowa, and the 126th became the first operational ANG KC-97 "Stratotanker" squadron in December 1963.

Michigan was the second state to have F-89s assigned to their Air National Guard squadrons. They also were the largest recipient of them, with all three of their squadrons equipped with Scorpions for a two year period.

53-2536 at General Mitchel Field, Milwaukee, Wisconsin. The boarding ladder seems redundant in light of the built in kicksteps. - Bob Burgess via Dave Ostrowski

50-795 had been one of the F-89Cs assigned to the 6520th Test Squadron at Hanscomb AFB under Project ARD-3F-602. Returned to interceptor configuration, it was assigned to the 172nd FIS at Battle Creek, Michigan. -Art Krieger via Paul Stevens

On June 6, 1955, the 172nd Fighter Bomber Squadron at Kellogg Field, Battle Creek, Michigan, converted from F-86s to F-89Cs and became designated as a fighter interceptor squadron. At this time they were under the command of Captain Chester Douglass. (Rank escalation had not yet reached the ANG, and many of their squadron commanders were still Captains, whereas in the regular Air Force, many were Lt. Colonels.)

The 172nd's actual conversion from Sabres to Scorpions had commenced in April with the arrival of their first F-89C. However, the transition was not a smooth one, as immediately after their redesignation to a FIS all of the Scorpions were grounded pending an engine modification. By the end of the year only seven of the aircraft had been modified, and seventeen more were awaiting parts.

On April 15, 1956, the 110th Fighter Group (Air Defense) was activated with Lt. Colonel Robert Flagg commanding. Flagg, who had been the commander of the 172nd Fighter Squadron prior to Douglass, moved up to command the 127th Fighter Interceptor Group at Romulus. Soon after this action had taken place Lt. Colonel Flagg rejoined the USAF as a liaison officer and was replaced by Major Percy Lewis as 110th FG commander.

During field training in 1957 Lt. John Myers and R/O Captain Richard Colburn won the Robert Welsh Memorial Trophy for excellence in air-to-air gunnery in their F-89.

On April 11, 1958, the 110th FG(AD) was inactivated and on the following day the 172nd FIS was redesignated as the 172nd Tactical Reconnaissance Squadron. The F-89Cs were flown to Davis-Monthan AFB for storage, and later salvage, and the 172nd equipped with RB-57As.

A gaggle of Scorpions sounds like a misnomer! Note the number of empty back seats, as the 172nd FIS had a difficult time recruiting radar observers. The 172nd FIS switched from F-86Es to F-89Cs on April 1955, and then to RB-57As in the Spring of 1958. -Col. Bob Stone via Mike Fox

51-5819 on the slush covered ramp of the 107th FIS at Detroit Wayne-Major Airport. It had previously served with the 74th FIS. -William J. Balogh, Sr. via Col. Bob Stone and Mike Fox

F-89Cs of the 107th FIS in their early paint scheme. These were ex 433rd FIS Scorpions. The 107th flew the F-89C from June 1955 until February 1958. -Col. Bob Stone via Mike Fox

Michigan's 107th FIS used yellow as their squadron color. 51-5813 had previously served with the 433rd FIS, and it went to Davis Monthan AFB for storage and later salvage in May 1958 when the 107th converted to RF-84F/Ks and changed roles. -via Doug Barbier

At Detroit Wayne-Major Airport, the 107th Fighter Bomber Squadron and 171st Fighter Interceptor Squadron had both been flying F-86Es since the summer of 1953 after conversion from F-51Hs. In June 1955 both squadrons switched to F-89Cs and the 107th FBS was redesignated as a FIS. Both the 107th and 171st FISs were under the control of the 127th Fighter Interceptor Wing at Wayne-Major Airport, which was commanded by Colonel Magus Marks. Merwin Reed led the 107th FIS, while Clay Hedges commanded the 171st.

The majority of the 107th FIS F-89Cs came from the 74th FIS at Thule Air Base, while those assigned to the 171st had been previously been assigned to the 433rd FIS at Ladd AFB. All of these had undergone IRAN (Inspect and Repair as Necessary) rework at Ogden Air Material Area at Hill AFB, Utah, prior to delivery to Detroit. The exceptions were a half dozen that came from Wisconsin 176th FIS that were surplus to their requirements.

A nice profile shot of a 107th FIS F-89C in the squadron's later paint scheme. 51-5800 had previously belonged to the 176th FIS. The F-89C cost $797,202.00, which included engines, electronics, ordnance and armament. -A/2c Menard via Col. Bob stone and Mike Fox

In February 1958 the 171st FIS switched to Republic RF-84F Thunderstreaks, and the 107th FIS followed suit in April. On April 12 both squadrons were redesignated as Tactical Reconnaissance. All of their F-89Cs were then flown to Davis-Monthan AFB for storage and later salvage.

Idaho's 190th Fighter Interceptor Squadron at Boise had been flying F-94A and Bs as an interim interceptor after re-equipping from F-86As in November 1953. In April 1956 they received ex-Wisconsin F-89Bs to replace the F-94s, and expanded to Fighter Interceptor Group size with the activation of the 124th Fighter Interceptor Group.

In April 1959 the 190th FIS converted to F-86Ls and their F-89Bs were flown to Davis-Monthan AFB for salvage. The 190th FIS was the last F-89B squadron.

The 186th FIS is assigned to the Montana Air National Guard as their sole ANG squadron. Their transition record was similar to that of Idaho's, having switched from Sabres to F-94As, and then to F-89Cs in April 1956. The unit was also expanded upon receipt of the Scorpion, and the 120th Fighter Interceptor Group was activated at Great Falls Municipal Airport.

The majority of the F-89Cs came directly from the 126th FIS at Milwaukee, Wisconsin, while the remainder were ex-57th FIS Scorpions that had been returned from Iceland and gone through IRAN before assignment to the 186th.

In August 1958 the F-89Cs were sent to Arizona for disposal and replaced by F-89Hs for an eighteen month period, and then F-89Js were obtained. One of these Js was destroyed on March 22, 1962, after a fuel system failure. Its pilot was trying to get it back, but hit the ground while in a turn. The crew did survive. In July 1966 the 186th FIS converted to F-102As.

Down in the rough. Capt. Edward Russ of the 107th FIS was faced with an emergency landing with an unsafe landing gear indication, which turned out to be true when the gear collapsed. -Col. Bob Stone via Mike Fox

Incident: Captain Victor Kaltoff was first in line for takeoff of the entire 171st FIS from Detroit Wayne Major. He lost an engine and "ditched" in the field at the end of the runway. The Scorpion was repaired and served with the 171st until December 1957. -Col. Bob Stone via Mike Fox

The 123rd Fighter Interceptor Squadron is based at Portland Municipal Airport. In June 1957 the 123rd FIS was the first ANG squadron to transition from F-94Bs to F-89Ds. However, they only flew the F-89D for six months before switching to F-89Hs. The F-89Hs arrived in November 1957 and they were in the 123rd's inventory longer than any other unit until September 1960. At this time the 123rd FIS was commanded by Lt. Colonel Patrick O'Grady, while the parent 142nd FIG was led by Lt. Colonel Waldo Timm.

In September the Hs were replaced by F-89Js, of which they lost four in operational accidents. The first took place on February 25, 1961, after its crew ejected after loosing its attitude gyro during instrument flight. Their second loss was on December 26, 1962, when the F-89 caught fire in flight and its crew had to abandon it. The ejection was successful, but the aircraft did destroy a house when it crashed. Their third F-89 loss was on June 6, 1964, when an engine exploded on

Another F-89C of the 107th FIS, with its new paint scheme half applied. A Dash 35 model, it did not have the large purge generators of the previous C models. -A/2c Menard

takeoff, but its crew got out okay. Their last loss occurred on November 25, 1964, during a landing incident, and once again its crew was unhurt.

In January 1966 the 123rd FIS obtained F-102As from the 460th FIS that was in the process of being inactivated at Portland.

Washington's 116th Fighter Interceptor Squadron had also been flying F-94s. Based at Geiger Field, Spokane, the 116th FIS received F-89Ds in October 1957. On July 1, 1960, the 116th FIS was expanded to Group size with the activation of the 141st Fighter Interceptor Group, with Lt. Colonel Wilson Gillis selected as the new Group Commander.

The parent 142nd FIW, which included Oregon's 123rd FIS, was commanded by Colonel Frank Frost at the time, but he passed away in May 1961 and was replaced by Lt. Colonel Gillis. Major Lloyd Howard replaced Gillis as 141st FIG commander at this time, and he held the position until 1963 when Lt. Colonel Lyle Scott was selected to it.

In June 1960 the F-89Ds gave way to F-89Js, and then the 116th FIS started to have real problems, losing one a year. On December 28, 1961, one crashed during an instrument approach and its crew was killed. On January 4, 1962, another F-89J exploded in flight and its pilot was killed. Another was lost on November 14, 1963, when its pilot lost control of the aircraft during a night practice intercept mission, but the crew ejected okay. Their last F-89 was lost on January 31, 1964, when it skidded off the runway.

In August 1965 the 116th FIS converted to F-102As.

On the East Coast, the 132nd Fighter Interceptor Squadron at Dow AFB, Bangor, Maine, converted from F-94Bs to F-89Ds in September 1957. The "Maineiacs" flew the D model until December 1959 when they were replaced by F-89Js received from the 319th FIS at Bunker Hill AFB when that squadron converted to F-106s. The 132nd FIS expanded to

Showing some evidence of having fired its cannons, 49-2467 of the 190th FIS taxies in for parking. The F-89B in the background, 49-2443, was the last operational loss of a B model Scorpion, crashing in May 1959. -Isham Collection

Idaho was the last user of the cannon-armed F-89s, not retiring them until December 1959. By the time the 190th got them, they were already hand-me-downs from Wisconsin and Michigan. -Isham Collection

Group size on December 1, 1960, with the reactivation of the 101st FIG.

The 132nd was the largest ANG F-89J squadron, possessing twenty-eight examples, of which two were lost. On June 4, 1966, one F-89J exploded in flight, killing one crew member, while the other survived. On November 23, 1968, another F-89 exploded on the ground while it was being prepared for a practice mission. No one was injured. In July 1969 the 132nd FIS switched to F-102As, with the distinction of being the last USAF/ANG Scorpion squadron.

Back in the Mid West, the 109th FIS, based at Holman Field, St. Paul, Minnesota, was operating under trying conditions.

The F-94As and Bs that they had obtained from their sister squadron, the 179th FIS, were having a hard time operating from the short Holmon runways. While satisfactory for their earlier Mustangs, they were unsuitable for extensive jet operations, so the squadron had to spend a lot of their time on the road or flying back and forth to the (then) ANG summer training camp at Volk Field, Wisconsin, to conduct their training.

On January 2, 1958, the USAF inactivated the 432 FIS at Wold-Chamberlain Airport, Minneapolis, and the 109th FIS obtained their inventory "lock, stock and barrel," including their F-89Hs.

With the 109th FIS commanded by Lt. Colonel Marvin Thorson and the parent 133rd FIG commanded by Colonel Edmund Antonini, the 109th FIS flew the Scorpion until January 1960 when their mission changed to that of an air transport squadron and they obtained C-97As. The 109th FIS had been the only ANG squadron to fly only the F-89H version.

Further to the west, South Dakota's 175th FIS at (Joe) Foss Field, Sioux Falls, was the flying unit of the 114th FIG, commanded by Colonel Duane Corning. In January 1958 the

175th FIS began conversion to F-89Ds from F-94Cs, which took them until May to complete the change to Scorpions.

In the early part of 1960 the 175th FIS started a conversion to F-89Js which was never completed, because in the fall of the same year they surrendered their Scorpions to Davis-Monthan and transitioned to F-102As.

Vermont's "Green Mountain Boys," the 134th FIS, was the next ANG squadron to transition from F-94s to F-89Ds. In April 1958 their F-94s were either sent to Davis-Monthan AFB for storage/salvage, or to other ANG squadrons. Major Richard Mock was the squadron commander. Mock had four kills while flying with the 317th Fighter Squadron during WWII, and then had spent fourteen months as a POW after being shot down over Hungary.

In January 1960 the 134th FIS began to participate in the ADC's runway alert program. From a half hour before sun-

One of the few F-89Cs originally delivered to the 74th FIS before the series of accidents forced their recall for refurbishment, 51-5794 later served with the 57th FIS at Keflavik, and then went to Montana's 186th FIS. -Dave Ostrowski

Montana's 186th FIS replaced their F-89Cs with F-89Hs in August 1958, and the H model gave way to J models in March 1960. In July 1966 their Scorpions were retired and replaced by F-102s. -Frank MacSorley

Out to pasture, 51-11381, a F-89D that had previously belonged to the 116th FIS awaits its turn to be salvaged at Davis Monthan AFB, Arizona, in April 1960. Countless aircraft have gone through this facility, which has saved millions of dollars while in the process of reclaiming worthwhile material while scraping the rest. -Doug Olson

rise until a half hour after sunset, a F-89 would be parked off the end of the instrument runway with a crew strapped-in the cockpit and awaiting scramble orders In June 1960 their older F-89Ds gave way to later block F-89Ds and Js from the 59th FIS that was switching to F-102s at Goose Bay, Newfoundland. A month later the 158th Fighter Group (Air Defense) was federally recognized with Lt. Colonel Robert Goyette as group commander. At this time the 134th FIS went on full time, twenty-four hour alert status.

In October 1962 the Vermont ANG was awarded the Operational Readiness Award by the National Guard Bureau

Newly assigned F-89Ds to replace their F-94s, the 116th FIS at Geiger Field, Spokane, Washington, obtained these Scorpions in the Fall of 1957. These early block Ds, not being modified to J standards were simply phased out in the late 1950s and early 1960s. -Washington ANG photo via Doug Olson

for having the highest degree of readiness of any ANG F-89 squadron.

On March 4, 1965, (now) Colonel Robert Goyette and 1st Lt. Jeffrey Pollock were killed while returning from a training sortie. Their F-89 had caught fire and crashed two miles south of the Ethan Allan AFB runway. Lt. Colonel John McHugo was named the new 158th FG(AD) commander.

In August of 1965 the 134th FIS received F-102s.

Back in the Mid West, once again, the 178th FIS at Hector Field, Fargo, North Dakota, switched to F-89Ds in December 1958, with the "Happy Hooligans" F-94Cs being sent to Davis- Monthan in June 1959. Five months later the F-89Ds were replaced by F-89Js.

The 178th FIS, which had expanded to be a portion of the 119th FIG during their Starfire era, continued with the Scorpion until November 1966 when they were replaced by F-102s.

In March 1959 the 103rd FIS at Greater Pittsburgh, Pennsylvania, received F-89Hs from the 75th FIS at Dow AFB when that squadron converted to F-101Bs. At this time the 103rd FIS came under the 111th FIG and the 112th FIW, with the Wing commanded by Colonel Edgar Owen.

The 103rd FIS's F-94Cs were sent to Davis-Monthan AFB during the early summer months, and as the F-89Hs were slow in arriving, their first summer encampment was accomplished with limited aircraft resources. On January 1, 1960, the 103rd FIS was able to commence daylight ADC runway alert status with their Scorpions.

In January 1961 the 103rd FIS replaced their F-89Hs with F-89Js, with most of these coming from the 76th FIS. With the J model they had two major accidents. On January 25, 1961, one of the aircraft that had been used to develop the wingtip armament configuration for the F-89H, but had been retrofitted to F-89J standards, 53-2449, caught fire on takeoff from Greater Pittsburgh. The pilot attempted to turn the aircraft away from a populated area, but lost control and crashed resulting in two people being killed. The other accident involved an aborted takeoff that sheared the nose landing gear.

On April 1, 1962, the 111th FIG was retasked as an Air Transport Group and they replaced their Scorpions with C-97s. At this time they were relieved from the 112th FIW and assigned to the 118th Air Transport Wing, Tennessee ANG.

In July 1959 the 179th FIS at Duluth IAP, Minnesota, was under the command of Lt. Colonel Wayne Gatlin and they switched from F-94Cs to F-89Js. The following July the 148th FIG was activated at Duluth under Colonel Ralph Jerome, who had been the commanding officer of the 179th FIS prior to and just after their Korean Conflict service.

As soon as their aircrews were qualified in the Scorpion, the 179th FIS went on a twenty-four hour alert configuration to bolster the Northern Tier's defense perimeter.

1964 was the busiest year for the 179th FIS and the F-89. On October 28 they had their only major accident with the aircraft was when one departed K. I. Sawyer AFB, Michigan, after a refueling stop. Its fire warning lights came on just as the aircraft broke ground, and smoke entered the cockpit, which was followed by both engines starting to vibrate in their mounts. The pilot, flying solo, ejected successfully, although he did have burns from the flames that had started to enter the cockpit. Also in 1964 the 179th FIS won the Ricks Trophy Race, an ANG competition.

In November 1966 the 179th FIS switched to F-102As.

The last Air National Guard squadron to receive the F-89 was the 124th FIS of the Iowa ANG. The 124th FIS transitioned from F-86Ls to F-89Js at Des Moines in April 1962, receiving their Scorpions from the 126th FIS at Milwaukee, Wisconsin, when that squadron converted to KC-97s.

Immediately thereafter the 124th FIS received their second Winston P. Wilson Award for excellence as an ADC squadron and then an additional two more awards from the Na-

52-1849 of the 132nd FIS. It had previously been assigned to the 319th FIS. Note the plexiglas windscreen in front of the RO's position, to protect him from excessive windblast if the canopy was lost in flight. -Barry Miller

tional Guard Bureau for their successful transition in mission aircraft. Continuing in this tradition, the 124th FIS received the Air Defense Command's "A" Award for the period July 15, 1964-July 15, 1965 and followed it up with another for the period July 15, 1965-July 15, 1966, becoming the first ANG unit with an ADC commitment to win two consecutive "A" Awards. Also, during 1965 they received their first Outstanding Unit Award, which was followed by a second one in 1968. Unfortunately they did lose one F-89 on December 9, 1968, when it crashed on a night interception mission and both crew members were killed.

In August 1969 the 124th FIS switched to F-84Fs and became a Tactical Air Command "gained" unit with their mission changing to close air support and interdiction. (From personal experience the author can state that the 124th FIS was one "Serria Hotel" F-89 squadron—which is Air Force jargon for "super hot.")

The first of the F-89D-35s, 52-1829, later became a J model. It was assigned to the 132nd FIS from the 319th FIS at Bunker Hill AFB, Indiana, when that squadron got F-106s. -Isham Collection

A nice profile shot of the same 132nd FIS F-89J, 52-2161, getting ready to depart Westover AFB, Massachussets, on May 16, 1964. -Tom Hildreth

A 175th FIS over South Dakota. For a period of time the 175th used "SODAK" as a radio call-sign, while the 178th FIS used "NODAK," which often created a terrific amount of radio confusion. -South Dakota ANG photo

One of the early F-89Ds assigned to the 175th FIS at Foss Field, Sioux Falls, South Dakota. The USAF and the ANG could not quite agree to who the ANG belonged to for a period, hence the abbreviated Air Force National Guard. Their squadron insignia, "Lobo," has since been revised to a frontal view, and "Lobo" became their radio call-sign. - Paul Stevens

One of the "Green Mountain Boys." The 134th FIS commenced twenty-four hour alert duties in 1960 and continued this air defense program through their F-102 era. 52-1906 had previously belonged to the 82nd and 59th FIS's. -Vermont ANG photo via Norm Taylor/Doug Olson

52-1888 had previously served with the 57th, 318th, 75th, and 59th FISs. It finally was assigned to Vermont's 134th FIS in June 1960. -via Tom Cuddy

Out to pasture at Davis-Monthan AFB, 52-2127 sits forelornly awaiting the scrappers torch among its contemporaries. The black square on the wing's leading edge is the ILS glide slope antenna. -Roger Besecker

After service with the 61st FIS at Earnst Harmon AB and the 59th FIS at Goose Bay AB, 52-2133 was assigned to Vermont's 134th FIS. Maximum takeoff weight of the Scorpion was 45,575 pounds, the heaviest of any fighter of its era. -Isham Collection

The first F-89D-45, 52-2127, which later became a F-89J. Its original "owner" was the 59th FIS at Goose Bay AB, and its last the 134th FIS. -Esposito

One of the last F-89Ds, a -75. Why these were not converted to J models is known only to the Air Force. 54-191 had originally been assigned to the 433rd FIS and then finished out its career with Vermont's 134th FIS. -via David Menard

53-2597 bearing the original markings of the 178th FIS, a carry-over from the scheme applied to their previous F-94s. Barely discernible on the radar dome is the anti-ice nozzle that could be used to spray deicer fluid on the dome if required. -McLaren Collection

Loading a Genie on a 178th FIS F-89J at Hector Field, Fargo, North Dakota. The wingtip fuel tank placement of the squadron insignia has given way to fluorescent paint in a 1958 anti-collision program. The size of the missile is evident. -North Dakota ANG via Doug Slowiak

With its arrestor barrier hook appearing almost obscene, 53-2604 of the 178th FIS. Note that the RO has his radar scope up and in place. -McLaren Collection

53-2610 of "NODAK's" 178th FIS. The added "0" prefix to the aircraft's serial number was added to denote that the aircraft was over ten years old. -A. Hafter via Esposito

In the final variation of the 178th FIS F-89 paint scheme, the "Happy Hooligans" motif was carried over to the later F-102s, and succeeding squadron interceptors. The 178th is one of the premier interceptor squadrons, having won the William Tell Meet four times and the Hughes Trophy twice. -ND ANG photo via Doug Slowiak

Pennsylvania's 103rd FIS had been one of the last ANG squadrons to fly the F-94C before switching to a combination of F-89Hs and Js in March 1959. Note that the FOD screens are in place while this well-worn H model is being taxied. -Esposito

54-385, a F-89H of the 103rd FIS. The 103rd started participating in the ADC runway alert program while flying F-94Cs and continued through their Scorpion era. -Esposito

With its boarding ladder and chocks still in place, this "come-on" is obviously staged. The F-89 had a well deserved reputation of being the world's largest vacuum cleaner, hence the intake screens on even the blow-in doors. -Isham Collection

A F-89J of the 103rd FIS. Previously this Scorpion had been a part of NEAC's 1956 Rocket Team as a D model. -Esposito

A well-worn 54-385 of the 103rd FIS, the last major operator of the F-89H with a bunch of the required sundry equipment: ground wires, fire bottle, canvas and wire intake screens, etc. The wingtank fuel caps are open to vent the single-point refueling system.-David Menard

52-1912 of the 124th FIS with interim markings and before ADC grey became the norm. In the background are the Sabre Dogs being replaced by the Scorpion in November 1962. -Iowa ANG via Doug Olson

53-2652 of the Des Moines, Iowa, based 124th FIS. Note that the Falcon launch pylons have been removed from this J model, as was the case with most of the ANG squadrons since the Falcon was a failure as Scorpion armament. -Frank MacSorley

In 1969 the 124th FIS sent their F-89Js to the salvage yard and were then assigned to the Tactical Air Command as a fighter-bomber squadron. They received already worn out F-84Fs from the Illinois 169th Tactical Fighter Squadron in a move that did not set well with either squadron, as the 169th then got the lowly Cessna U-3A "Blue Canoe" as their mission aircraft. -Iowa ANG via Doug Olson

The first American all-weather fighter to be designed as such for this mission was Jack Northrop's P-61 Black Widow. This particular example, a B model, belonged to NACA. -NASA via Bob Burns

Appearing stubby in this view, the prototype XF-89 was first shown to the public during the Summer of 1948 and made its first flight on August 16. -Northrop Grumman Corp.

Obviously a staged scene, but interesting nevertheless. The long upswept aft fuselage and empennage made the name Scorpion apropos. Note the "bullet" modification to the horizontal stabilizer in one of Northrop's experiments to control the airflow over the control surfaces. -Northrop Grumman Corp.

On February 22, 1950, the XF-89, 46-678 shown here disintegrated on its 102nd flight killing Northrop flight engineer Arthur Turton, while their pilot, Charles Tucker was thrown clear and survived. -Northrop Grumman Corp.

The XF-89 and following models had an extremely thin wing for an aircraft of its general bulk. It utilized the NACA, 0009-64 airfoil. -Northrop Grumman Corp.

Preparations for flight of the prototype XF-89. Northrop test pilot Fred Bretcher made the first flight on August 16, 1948. The flight was terminated after only eleven minutes duration, due to leaks in the aircraft's hydraulic and fuel systems. -Northrop Grumman Corp.

Unleashing the awesome firepower of 104 2.75" HVARs. This YF-89D was lost in a crash at Edwards AFB on October 10, 1953. -Northrop Grumman Corp.

Resplendent in a high-visibility paint scheme, the YF-89D, neé F-89B 49-2463, over California. Modifications included a new nose that included a 263 gallon fuel tank instead of cannon armament and 600 pounds of ballast. The new wingtip rocket pods show residue from earlier rocket firing. -Northrop Grumman Corp.

49-2434 with the blunt nosed Martin D-4 20mm rotatable turret. Delivered to the USAF in January 1951, it was modified to become the first F-89B on November 6, and later reverted back to A standards and was redesignated as an EF-89A. It now resides at Lackland AFB, Texas. -C. Kaston

The prototype F-89H at Edwards AFB with its "barberpole" yaw and pitch probe. Its first flight was on October 26, 1955. -Bud Butcher

51-11320 of the 438th FIS on a visit to Nellis AFB, NV. This F-89 was destroyed on December 12, 1955, after it caught fire during an engine start. The nose art appears to be a cave man chasing a bear. -Keener via David Menard

Although never the most photogenic aircraft, this F-89D appears almost sleek in this view off the California coast while on an acceptance test flight. -Northrop Grumman Corp.

Bearing the green circled cross of the National Safety Council, this F-89D represents six months of accident free work by the "Norcrafters." Those same six months equated to an "extra," or free F-89 to the company and the U.S. taxpayers in terms of lost hour savings. -Northrop Grumman Corp.

F-89D-75s of the 76th FIS on a flight out of Presque Isle AFB. 54-221 was Lt. Colonel Walter Hardee's assigned Scorpion. -J. Kerr

54-333 from the 76th FIS at Pinecastle AFB. The 76th FIS had obtained this Scorpion from the 84th FIS. The tiptanks certainly could be used as billboards. -Ron Picciani Collection

53-2659 of the 321st FIS. She was destroyed on July 12, 1956. The pilot made a missed approach, and then the F-89 caught on fire. The pilot attempted another approach, but landed "hot and long" and the F-89 was destroyed off the end of the runway. -J. Ford via Menard

Already appearing worn, 54-282 of the 76th FIS at Pinecastle AFB, Florida, in May 1959, a month before they switched to F-89Js. - Ron Picciani

Ready for a Bear, or a Bull, NATO code names for Russian bombers, a F-89J armed with the new Genie and Falcon air-to-air rockets. Modelers might note that these are the correct colors for the missiles, as this particular cocked and ready aircraft belonged to the 449th FIS at Ladd AFB. -R. Diozzi via David Menard

52-1938, one of three F-89Ds pulled from Northrop's line to become a prototype YF-89H, takes to the air. Camera distortion makes the wings appear bowed. Note the mid-wing camera pods to record the firing of the Falcon missiles. This particular D/H model was later modified to J standards and served as such with both the 319th and 132nd FISs. -Northrop Grumman Corp.

Resplendent in their red flight jackets, a Northrop crew prepares to board a brand new F-89H for a demonstration flight. The pylon tanks held 301 gallons of fuel, of which 300 were useable. The tip tanks held 308 gallons, of which 306 were useable. -Northrop Grumman Corp.

A F-89D of the 76th FIS during a visit to Stewart AFB, New York, in May 1957. This example was the third from the last F-89D built and it was assigned to a Flight Commander, as evidenced by the single fuselage stripe. -Peter Kane

445th FIS F-89Ds on patrol over Lake Huron. The 445th switched from F-89Ds to Hs in March 1956, being the first ADC squadron to make this Scorpion conversion. The insignia on their Scorpions were the early markings of the 30th Air Division. -A. J. Miller via David Menard

A line-up of 465th Scorpions from Griffis AFB, New York. 53-2649 finished its career with the 176th FIS. The 465th represented the EADF in the F-89 category during the 1958 William Tell. -Isham Collection

53-2629 of the 437th FIS's "Green Flight." It was later transferred to the 175th FIS. Hal Morgan via Menard

A F-89H of the 437th FIS. The 437th flew the H model Scorpion from July 1956 until March 1958 when they switched to the J model. H models of fighters seem to be somewhat jinxed, as the P-51H and F-86H likewise also had very short firstline Air Force careers. -Norman Filer via Mike Dario

The insignia of the 437th FIS, which was officially approved on September 1, 1953, eleven months after the squadron was activated. -Norman Filer via Mike Dario

52-2638, a F-89D-65 with the 437th FIS's flamboyant markings. Later converted to a F-89J, she finished out her service life with the 123rd FIS. -Jerry Greer via Larry Davis

53-2639 over California's mountains on a cross-country mission. The 321st FIS flew F-89Ds from their activation on August 18, 1955, until the Spring of 1956 when they switched to F-89Hs. -USAF

Factory fresh and headed north to Alaska in November 1954, these F-89Ds were assigned to the 65th FIS, and both were later modified to J models, to serve with other squadrons. -Northrop Grumman Corp.

54-238 was a F-89D that was equipped with long range ferry tanks, as used on the F-89J, for its transfer to Kelavik and assignment to the 57th FIS. The configuration of these tanks on the aircraft can make the identification of the particular Scorpion model difficult. -Lt. Col. Steiger

Cold and bleak, or starkly pretty, depending upon your outlook, in this shot of the Elmendorf AFB ramp. Notice how the "Old Shakey" C-124s in the distance still seems to dwarf the F-89. -Norm Filer via Mike Dario

53-2509 as assigned to the 449th FIS at Ladd AFB, Alaska. -Richard Diozzi

52-1931 of the 449th FIS. This Scorpion got around quite a bit, for after assignment in Alaska it was converted to a J model, assigned to the 4750th ADW at Vincent AFB in a training role, and then in June 1960 assigned to the 126th FIS at Milwaukee. When the 126th converted to KC-97s she was transferred to the 124th FIS at Des Moines, Iowa. -Ron Picianni Collection

52-1947 bearing the 449th FIS gyrfalcon insignia on its vertical stabilizer. After conversion to a J model this Scorpion served with the 59th FIS at Goose Bay Air Base, and then the 134th FIS at Ethan Allen. -D. Larson

52-1925 with the 449th FIS. It finished its career under somewhat puzzling circumstances as it became one of a small batch of F-89Js that were assigned to the 136th FIG at Dallas, Texas, yet the Group and its 181st FIS were flying F-86Ds at the time, and no Texas ANG squadron ever flew the Scorpion. -D. Larson

F-89Cs of the 74th FIS at Thule Air Base. The majority of the C models were transferred to the Michigan Air National Guard when F-89Ds arrived. -J. Ford

A close up of the F-89D armament of a 74th FIS Scorpion. Frangible plastic caps covered each rocket tube and prevented the free-floating rockets from sliding out under hard braking or other abrupt stopping conditions, and also helped keep moisture out of the launching tubes. -via Menard

The 74th FIS flightline at Thule Air Base, Greenland. The construction of Thule cost the US taxpayer 220 million in real dollars, and it was just 900 miles from the North Pole. -Lt. Col. Mike Martinolich

A close-up of the nose of 53-2599 of the 74th FIS. To the individual's right are the power receptacles while just to his left are vortex generators to stabilize the airflow into the engine intake. Above the "Mommie" is the right main (nose) fuel tank receptacle, which held 263 gallons of fuel. -via David Menard

An acceptance of a F-89 by a 74th FIS crew at Hawthorne, California, after ferrying back their C models in exchange. As a point of fact, the aircraft were usually referred to as simply '89s, with the given name of "Scorpion" being used only by flacks. These were all Block 60 versions, which were later modified to J standards. -Northrop Grumman Corp.

Chapter Five: Air Training Command

The primary recipient of the early F-89Cs was the 3625th Combat Crew Training Wing, CCTW, at Tyndall AFB, Panama City, Florida. Their early Scorpions arrived in December 1951 and most remained with the 3625th CCTW until the end of December 1953 and January 1954 when they were reassigned to the AAC or NEAC.

The Air Training Command complex at Tyndall during this period of time was one of the largest USAF facilities, with the 3625th CCTW being one of the largest Wings. The Wing itself was broken down into segments which included the 3625th Training Group (Interceptor, Air Crew), with this Group further broken down into squadrons devoted to the specific training of F-86D pilots, F-94 and F-89 pilots, and Radar Observers, ROs. (It should be noted that over the years the identification given to the "back seaters" in Air Force fighters progressed from Radio Operators, as initially their tasks stemmed from the operation of the radio and then expanded to include radar when it became operational. Radar, an acronym for 'radio' detection and ranging. The title/position progressed through Radar Observer, Radar Intercept Officer, etc). Additional assigned squadrons conducted the training of Ground Control Intercept officers ("Radar Wizards") and enlisted men ("Scope Dopes").

During the summer of 1953 the mission of training the all-weather fighter crews began to be relocated to Moody AFB, Valdosta, Georgia, as Tyndall was becoming too crowded with all of these other programs. At Moody, the new unit was the 3550th Combat Crew Training Wing, which included the 3553rd Combat Crew Training Squadron that was dedicated to training F-89 crews. They received some of the later F-89Cs, which were then sent to operational squadrons along with their crews when the first classes were graduated, then these C models were replaced with early block F-89Ds.

For preparation as a F-89 pilot or RO, classroom training started with an assignment to either Harlingen AFB, Texas, and the 3610th Navigator Training Wing or Ellington AFB, near Houston, and the 3605th Navigator Training Wing. At Ellington, classes were on navigation techniques and electronics in all forms, with emphasis on radar, celestial, dead reckoning, polar navigation and the proper use of navigational aids. Additional courses were heavy on meteorology, as this was obviously a key point for the all-weather fighter crews. Every facet of weather had to be thoroughly understood, including pressure patterns: "From High to Low, look out below..." as the all-weather interceptor crews were expected to be able to fly in any weather condition without regard to takeoff or landing minimums.

Pilot graduates from Ellington moved on to James Connelly AFB, Waco, Texas, and assignment to the 3565th Navigator Training Wing. Some went into B-47s where they became "triple threats," navigators, radar navigators, and electronic weapons officers. Those selected for assignment to

Bearing a non-standard placement of the F-89 " buzz letters" (and numbers), 53-2575 was assigned to the Air Training Command and the 3550th CCTW. If the aircraft was low enough for an observer to read these buzz letters, it was too low and pilots were probably in violation of safety regulations. -Isham Collection

Between June 21 and 26, 1954, the Air Defense Command flew the first World Wide air-to-air rocket meet at Yuma AFB, Arizona. These F-89Ds represented Moody's 3550th CCTW and the Air Training Command, but they did not compete for scoring. The tip tank rocket pods are blue with white stars. -USAF

The flightline at Yuma AFB, Arizona, during the 1955 Rocket Meet. The B-29s in the background were used as target tugs. -USAF

Colonel Carroll McColpin (pilot) and Lt. Kenneth Watson (radar observer). McColpin was the 64th AD's and NEAC's commander, and thus team captain for the October 1956 Rocket Meet at Vincent AFB. -USAF

all-weather fighters, as well as the future radar officers, also assigned to James Connelly from Ellington, commenced initial training in TB-25Ks and TB-25Ms, the WWII Mitchell bomber modified by Hughes Aircraft Corporation to become an airborne radar trainer with the Hughes E-1 or E-5 systems, respectively.

Training in these TB-25s was not considered to be "good duty," as the primary training position was located behind the bomb bay in the old waist gunners position, an extremely noisy location. There were three radar scopes in this area, one for the primary student, one for the instructor, and the third for a second student to monitor what the primary student was attempting while awaiting his turn in "the pit." A third student rode in the nose to act as an extra set of eyes to preclude a collision and monitor the interception.

Picking up pointers, 51-11398 and 53-2673 belonged to the Alaskan Air Command's 10th AD, and they are eavesdropping on a 64th AD mission brief prior to the 1956 ADC Rocket Meet at Vincent AFB. 53-2673 was later transferred to the 26th AD and it crashed on November 10, 1959, while penetrating a severe storm while on an interception mission. Both crew members were killed. -USAF

From James Connelly pilots and ROs moved to Moody AFB and the 3550th Combat Crew Training Wing for the final melding of the pilots and ROs as an interceptor team. Assignment to the F-89 program was not considered to be a happy choice, as the aircraft's reputation had not only presaged it, but the F-89 was also garnering a bad name at Moody with a high attrition rate in crews and aircraft. One dangerous maneuver that was initially required to be demonstrated was that of the split-ess, at night and on instruments, which resulted in some "spectacular nose dives straight into the swamp." This requirement was later removed from the curriculum.

In late 1956 both the F-89 and F-94 gunnery and rocket proficiency training programs that had also been conducted at Moody AFB were relocated to Yuma County Airport, Arizona, where the 4750th Training Wing (Air Defense) was based. The curriculum remained the same, but came under some trying times during the periods of summer heat as flying could only be conducted during the early morning hours or in the early evening. It often got so hot that the asphalt would give way under the heavy F-89s, and the runway became far too short for safe takeoffs or landings in the ambient air conditions.

The 4750th Training Wing, which later became an Air Defense Wing, was also responsible for operating the Air Defense Command's air-to-air gunnery and rocket firing ranges. All ADC pilots or crews were expected to fly forty air-to-air gunnery or rocket missions per year, and squadrons were rotated to Yuma/Vincent from their home bases to conduct these operations. The 4750th also ran and hosted the annual air defense aerial gunnery and rocketry competitions

Everyone turns out to witness the arrival of the first F-89J to be assigned to the 4750th Air Defense Squadron (Weapons) at Vincent AFB. It still has the D wingtanks, which were changed by the gaining unit. The B-57 in the background was used for high altitude target towing. - Isham Collection

between 1953 and 1956. (There was no meet in 1957. In 1958 the competition was moved to Tyndall AFB.)

In June 1957 the Advanced Phase of the navigator-radar interceptor course moved to James Connelly from Moody AFB and brought about the transfer of all of Moody's F-89s to James Connelly. In 1959 the F-89 training program was transferred entotal to James Connelly and 3550th PTW assumed responsibility for training both USAF and ANG crews until the program was phased out at the end of the Scorpion's career.

Chapter Six: Test Missions

Strangely enough, considering the large wing on the F-89 and its ability to mount several underwing pylons and equipment, or the large cannon bay on the early models (the avionics bay in the later versions), the F-89 was never utilized to any major extent or capacity in a test/evaluations or research role, in contrast to all other USAF fighters in its era.

In fact, the F-89 was the only major fighter never to have been assigned to the National Advisory Committee for Aeronautics, NACA, which later became NASA. The only example, 49-2425, ever being furnished to NACA was a "loaner" from the USAF's All-Weather Flying Center that was further placed on bailment to the Lightning and Transient Research Institute at Minneapolis, Minnesota, to evaluate the effects of artificial lightning strikes of some 200,000 amperes on the aircraft's electrical and fuel systems. These were all ground tests in static conditions, conducted under the auspices of the Air Material Command.

Cold weather testing is conducted on all Air Force aircraft for obvious reasons. The Air Force was particularly interested in the F-89's ability to withstand the cold, as it was initially slated for assignment to Alaska, northern Maine, and the Northeast Air Command, all climates of extreme cold and involving rugged topography, where its range and twin-engine reliability was an absolute necessity.

Initially one of the early F-89Cs was assigned for these tasks, 50-743, that went to Eglin AFB and assignment to the 3202nd Test Group. At Eglin, the F-89 was placed in their cold-weather hanger, and the temperatures lowered in increments to -65 degrees, to ascertain all systems reliability in static conditions. Then this F-89 was flown to Ladd AFB for operational suitability tests in conditions down to an actual -54 degrees. It was not the actual cold that caused problems with the F-89, but temperature fluctuations, as they ranged as much as forty-eight degrees in a twelve hour period. There were leaks found in all systems, but these were easily dealt with as far as determining the problem and the method to fix it was concerned. It was the actual mechanical repair work that was the hazard, as maintenance personnel had to wear three pairs of gloves at a time—nylon, wool and leather—or lined mittens in order to work in the frigid conditions. A dropped tool or part in the snow was hard to find and pick up, and one did not dare to attempt to do so with out hand protection. Most of the actual outdoor maintenance hours had to be spent in front of Herman-Nelson heaters to warm the men. Lt. Colonel Victor Curtiss was the Project Officer on this effort.

Other F-89s were run through similar cold weather tests, although most of these were conducted at Eglin on specific aircraft or equipment, as each item added to the aircraft had to be certified that it would function in the cold before it was placed in service. F-89D 52-1836 was utilized for many of these tests before eventual assignment to Presque Isle and the 74th FIS.

Notwithstanding the F-89's lack of use in ancillary development programs, it was utilized extensively by the Air Force and subcontractors to either enhance existing armament systems or develop new ones, either for upcoming F-89s or other types of aircraft.

One of the first of these programs was the development and feasibility studies of the Martin Aircraft Corporation D-1 Fire Control System. This system had been originally intended for both the F-87 and the F-89, had the former remained in contract. The D-1 System was composed of four 20mm cannons installed in a turret to be mounted in the nose of these aircraft, with the capability to be swiveled 360 degrees and elevated to 105 degrees. This would permit the cannons to maintain direct fire upon a target while in a rapidly changing relationship to the interceptor.

The test vehicle for this system was F-89A 49-2434 which was assigned to the 2750th Test and Evaluations Group at Wright-Patterson AFB, Ohio, on March 2, 1951, long after the F-87 program had been dropped. Although demonstrated as operationally viable during ground tests, the rotating turret created a terrific amount of aerodynamic unstability when-

52-1834 spent a short period with the 4750th Test Squadron at Tyndall AFB, Florida, after conversion from a D to a J model Scorpion to conduct armament tests. -via G. Olvera

OPPOSITE: 49-2475 served under several designations. An EF-89B, EF-89A, JF-89B, and finally as a F-89B when it was retired from its test programs and finally became operational as an interceptor with the 190th FIS. Here it is wearing the red with yellow trim paint scheme when it served with the All-Weather Flying Center. -Air Force Museum

F-89C 51-5795 was modified to carry the T-110E3 rocket launchers which fired T-131 2.75" spin-stabilized rockets from rifled barrels. Although fifty rockets could be carried, twice that of the F-86D, the later F-89D armament was deemed more effective. -Isham Collection

ever the cannons were rotated or elevated from straight ahead. In November 1951 this F-89A, since redesignated as an EF-89A, was returned to Northrop and its airframe improved to become the first of the F-89A to B conversions. Then, on December 22, 1951, its designation was revised back to that of the EF-89A once again, and it was returned to Wright-Patterson as a test aircraft. It remained there until eventual reassignment to the 4750th Training Wing at Yuma County Airport, Arizona, where it continued to be flown with the Martin turret and evaluated against towed targets. In August 1955 it was flown to Kelly AFB, San Antonio, Texas, where it was then towed to Lackland AFB to serve as a display aircraft.

There were several "Project Gun-Val" programs, one of which involved the F-86 conversion from .50 caliber machine guns to 20mm cannons for service in the Korean War. The F-94B with 20mm and 60mm cannons was another. The F-89s participation in "Gun-Val" involved F-89C's 51-5766 and -5772 which had four Swiss-made Oerlikon 302RX 30mm cannons installed, with 100 rounds each. These provided the heaviest firepower for any aircraft in this period in time, but they did not prove to be a feasible armament. Both aircraft's noses were changed back to those of the standard F-89C and the aircraft were later assigned to the Air National Guard's 126th and 186th FISs.

A F-89H assigned to the 3211st INT Test Group, Air Proving Ground Command, Eglin AFB, Florida. The pylon tanks under the wings have an unknown function. -Isham Collection

Let's not show the public everything. 50-794 had been lent to the 6520th Test Support Wing at Hanscom AFB for what was then the super secret "Cape Cod Project," hence the canopy was covered during an open house to keep curious eyes out of its cockpit. -Tom Cuddy

Another "Gun-Val" Scorpion was F-89C 51-5795, whose nose was modified to carry two T-110E3 rocket launchers. Each of these launchers were fed by a twenty-five rocket magazine that carried 2.75" folding-fin spin-stabilized rockets. The rockets were actually fired from rifled cannon barrels and ignited in flight. The tests were conducted by the Air Force Armament Center at Eglin AFB.

Another series of tests at Eglin involved the installation of a downward firing T-160 cannon to determine the effects of high-speeds and cross winds upon the ballistics of the projectile and the trajectories of defensive fire.

The Thieblot Aircraft Company built a special steel-beamed and reinforced nose for the subject F-89C that was a foot longer than the standard nose, designed to have absolutely no flexibility whatsoever. The cannon was fired from altitudes ranging between 15,000 and 40,000 feet at night in conjunction with four cameras on the aircraft and four on the ground, along with the newly developed Doppler radar for tracking, to determine the perfect accuracy of the shell. The results of these tests evolved into the defensive tail turret of the B-58.

50-800 was another Cape Cod Project F-89C. In June 1957 it was finally assigned to an operational squadron, the 186th FIS, and a year later it was flown to Arizona to be salvaged. -Air Force Museum

52-1831 had a most varied and traveled career. It had served with the 57th, 318th, 465th, 75th and 76th FIS's. In June 1961 it was transferred to the US Army's Missile Command, and, as seen here, on duty at Yokota Air Base, Japan, in May 1963 -A/1c Menard

At Hanscom AFB, Mass., the 6520th Test Support Wing had a half dozen F-89Cs delivered under project ARD-3F-602 in the Summer and Fall of 1953, and later another half dozen F-89Ds and Js for their test and evaluations programs. Many of these programs were involved with the "Cape Cod Project," the development of the Data Link system that became the basis of the SAGE system.

Conducted by the Lincoln Laboratory of the Massachusetts Institute of Technology, the Cape Cod Project started with F-89Cs 51-5845, -5847, and -5849 as testbeds for the installation of the Data Link radio equipment, which at that early time was a thirty-one digit time-division multiplex system in the UHF frequency ranges which gave an aircraft a discrete address by using the first four digits of each numerically coded word as the address. Five more F-89Cs were added to the program by October 1953, along with a F-94C and a pair of F3Ds. Although the Scorpions were the developmental aircraft in the Data Link program, it was intended

The one and only live firing of a nuclear armed Genie missile over the Nevada Test Range on July 19, 1957. Captain Eric Hutchison was the pilot and Captain Alfred "Cliff" Barbee was the Weapons Officer. - Northrop Grumman Corp.

for the single-pilot interceptors of the F-86L and F-102 ilk, and the equipment never saw operational usage in the F-89.

Likewise, at Vincent AFB, Arizona, the 4750th Training Wing (Air Defense, Weapons) was headquartered. (Nee Yuma County Airport and named for General Casey Vincent, who was the inspiration for the cartoon character "Steve Canyon.") This Wing had a similar numbered Group and Squadrons also based at Vincent, which in reality was one of the few Air Force bases run by fighter pilots for fighter pilots. Wing and base commander was Colonel (later General) Robert Worlet. Colonel Glenn Eagleston commanded the 4750th Group (18.5 air-to-air kills during WWII and two MiG 15s in Korea). Group Operations Officer was Colonel Vermont Garrison (7.3 kills in WWII and ten MiG 15s). Another example was Major James Jabara, who ran the F-86D squadron (1.5 kills during WWII and fifteen MiG 15s). The 4750th was responsible for all live air-to-air rocketry and cannon qualifications for Air Defense Command fighters, squadrons, and crews until the more sophisticated and longer ranged Falcon and Genie missiles came into use and required more geographical space than the Arizona Range had available and the entire operation had to be relocated to Tyndall AFB. The 4750th TW(AD,W) also included the 4750th Test Squadron which had a detachment at Griffiss AFB, New York. This detachment was involved with the development and then the operational testing and evaluation of the tracking systems for the XF-99 Bomarc antiaircraft missile. Several of the Griffiss based F-89s were later redesignated as DF-89s and transfered to the US Army.

Also joining the US Army were several ex-76th FIS F-89Js that also became DF-89s. These Scorpions were actually returned to Northrop on bailment, for use by the US Army Missile Command at primary bases at Ft. Bliss, Texas, Ft. Sill, Oklahoma, and Yokota Air Base, Japan. Further assign-

ment returned these aircraft to the USAF and took them to Clark Air Base, Philippine Islands. Eventually they were salvaged at Hickam AFB, Hawaii, as the most widely traveled F-89s built.

Flown by contracted civilian pilots, the DF-89s carried RP-76 drone targets for the Army's Nike missile batteries to track. The drones would be air launched, and the Nike site would locate and track the drone to the point of optimum interception, but the Nikes were not fired.

At Clark AB, under Project Charging Sparrow, DF-89Js of the USAF's 6400th Test Squadron launched RP-78 missiles as aerial targets for AIM-7 "Sparrows" fired by F-4Cs in an attempt to improve the reliability of the combination Phantom/Sparrow weapons system. Due to various problems, it was found that only 80% of the launched Sparrows were reliable, and only two-thirds of the evaluated F-4Cs were able to even launch the AIM-7 properly.

Perhaps the ultimate test of the 1950s and atomic weaponry was the "John Shot." Although Convair had demonstrated that an operating nuclear reactor could be carried aloft in one of their B-36s, and atomic bombs were being detonated on a regular schedule, the John Shot was the only actual detonation of an airborne atomic defensive missile.

As a portion of Operation Plumb Bob, a Genie rocket-powered MB-1 (later designated as the AIR-2A) was fired for the first and only time with its live warhead being detonated at 18,000 feet over the Atomic Energy Commission's Yucca Flats, Nevada, test center on July 19, 1957.

Although the nuclear capable F-89J had entered the USAF's inventory in the Fall of 1956 and the 84th FIS at Hamilton AFB had theoretically become operational with the Genie on December 31, the Genie itself had never been demonstrated.

In September 1956 Colonel John deVires was selected as the Project Officer for the John Shot, a super-sensitive mission commanded by Colonel Paul Wignall of the 4950th Test Group (Atomic) at Kirtland AFB, New Mexico. The primary aircrew selected was that of Captains Eric Hutchison and R/O Albert Barbee of the 84th FIS, while Lts. Burford Culpepper and R/O Jim Jones of the 445th FIS at Wurtsmith AFB were the alternate team. Lt. Robert Gee and Captain Al Moore from Wright Patterson AFB were the chase aircrew.

Originally it had been hoped to use either a F-102 or a F-101B for the John Shot, but the F-101B was not yet available from McDonnell and the F-102 would have required an extensive modification at the time to configure it to be able to launch the Genie, so the F-89J became the weapon of choice.

Initially an airborne target was desired, and several, all unsuitable, were offered. A drone F6F or QF-80C were considered as "hard" targets, while a legitimate drone, such as the Ryan Firebee, was too small. A QB-17 was rejected, as it simply did not fit the image—an antique WWII bomber being knocked down by an atomic age missile! A B-47 was offered, and accepted, but it would have required a crew of three to get it airborne and headed towards Yucca Flats before the

One of the chase F-89Hs assigned to Operation Plumb Bob and the John Shot was 54-409, which belonged to the 432nd FIS. For some reason it missed the mission, whose detonation is seen over the mountain range. The 432nd was inactivated in January 1958 and this just happens to be the only known photograph of one of their F-89Hs. -Northrop Grumman Corp.

crew bailed out, which was considered an acceptable risk. However, SAC immediately demanded that this aircraft not be used as it would have been extremely detrimental to the moral of their personnel to witness the demise of one of their first line bombers to an atomic defensive weapon.

In the end, it was decided to air-launch the Genie for an air-burst over the Yucca Flats range without any target at all. This was successfully accomplished as a "one time" effort on July 19. Although the Genie became the mainstay defensive weapon for many years, and many were fired as inert weapons for aircrew training, any additional live firing of the atomic warhead was deemed as too expensive and unnecessary. The point had been made and was believed to be well taken by potential aggressors.

A F-89J assigned to Operation Plumb Bob as a chase aircraft. It was flown by Lt. Robert Gee and Captain Al Moore, from Wright Patterson AFB. After involvement in so many atomic blasts it probably glowed in the dark. -Northrop Grumman Corp.

Chapter Seven: F-89 Proposals

As with any viable aircraft design, there is always further room for improvement on an existing product as ideas and technology evolve. Some of those ideas involving the F-89 were pretty much straightforward. Revisions in engines, avionics, armament systems and firepower were expected, as with any other type of aircraft.

The modification of 49-2463, a B model that became the prototype D model, is one example of this, as were the three later D models, 52-1830, -1938, and 53-2449 that became the test-beds for the development of the F-89H.

Falling somewhere between these two programs and Northrop's proposals for advanced technology fighters came the YF-89E, a F-89C-5 serialed 50-752, that was the first of two aircraft designs to bear the F-89E designation. This example was powered by two Allison YJ71-A-3 engines. The powerplants produced 9,700 pounds of static thrust without afterburners, approximately 3,000 pounds more than the standard J35-A33A installed in the F-89C. Initially tested under a B-45 in a pod that could be extended and then retracted from the Tornado's bomb bay, the YJ71 weighed 1,750 pounds more than the J35, and although smaller in diameter, it did require larger air intakes to feed the engine.

F-89C 50-752 was made available to the Air Force on November 29, 1951, but Northrop's development team held on to the aircraft for three years while waiting for the engines and preparing it for flight. The first flight of the YF-89E was not accomplished until June 10, 1954, at Hawthorne, and on August 30 it was delivered to Edwards AFB for further evaluation. Although the YJ71 engines were far more powerful than the J-35s, their additional weight was too much of a penalty and negated any benefit, so the program was terminated in 1955.

The second F-89E proposal fell somewhat along the lines of McDonnell's XF-88 and Lockheed's XF-90, being a design for an interim escort fighter, a role that was eventually filled by Republic's F-84Fs and Gs before this type of mission requirement was dropped by SAC.

This proposed F-89E had several obvious design differences from the operational models. It was to be a single seat fighter with a considerably shorter canopy over the cockpit, which was slightly aft of the usual position, a location that would not have improved visibility at all.

The wing of this proposed model, which actually preceded 50-572, resembled the previous wings in general plan form but was of an entirely new design that was 15.5% larger in wing area and was to have spanned 64', 5". In addition to wing-tip fuel tanks, two nacelles were to carry a standard armament of 104 2.75" FFARs, while the nose armament bay could be fitted with various packages of ten .50 caliber machine guns, six 20mm cannons, or six MX-904 guided missiles.

This F-89E version was to be powered by two J47-GE-21 turbojet engines, similar to those installed in F-86Ds, that produced 9,100 pounds thrust in afterburner. Fuel capacity was to be 3,000 gallons, over ten tons of fuel which was an unheard of amount at the time, which was to give the F-89E a 1,000 mile combat radius. The expectation was that it could reach 40,000 feet in seven minutes and operate at Mach .9.

Similar in fuselage arrangement was another version that was not given an official designation by Northrop. This was the swept-wing model that actually preceded the F-89E proposal and was based upon the F-89A. Northrop proposed that this aircraft would actually have minimal changes over the existing F-89A, stating that the new swept wing was only a modification of the existing wing, with the panels only swept back 35 degrees. The horizontal stabilizer was reduced by 25%. Two Allison 450E-1 engines that were to produce 10,000 pounds thrust (plus 50% more in afterburner) were to be installed. It was expected that these engines would give the Scorpion the ability to reach 35,000 feet in seven minutes, a combat ceiling of 65,000 feet at 661 mph, and a maximum speed of 731 mph at sea level. Armament was to be either 20mm cannons, or an arrangement of 2.75" HVARs around

Based upon the original F-89A design, the swept-wing modification was to be a point defense interceptor with a single cockpit. -Northrop Grumman Corp.

OPPOSITE: The F-89F "Interim Escort Fighter" was to be powered by two J-47-GE-21 engines that provided 9,100 pounds of static thrust. Its fuel capacity was to be expanded to 3,000 gallons, which was to have given the aircraft a 1,000 mile combat range. -Northrop Grumman Corp.

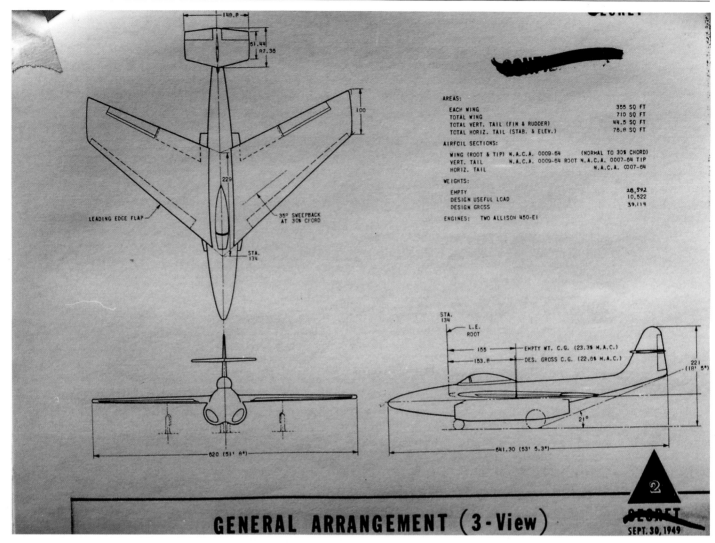

GENERAL ARRANGEMENT (3 - View)

SEPT. 30, 1949

The span of the swept-wing interceptor was to have been 51' 8" with a total wing area of 710 square feet. The length was 53' 5" and the height 18' 5". Empty weight was to be 28,592 pounds with a design gross weight of 39,114 pounds. -Northrop Grumman Corp.

the nose mounted radar, similar to the future F-94C. A photo-reconnaissance nose was also an option.

Another photo-reconnaissance version was a modification to the basic F-89A/B/C design which replaced the 20mm cannon armament with an array of cameras in the F-89s nose. In addition, replacing the wingtip fuel tanks were similar shaped pods that were to contain flash bombs and other sundry reconnaissance items. Instead of having conventional underwing fuel tanks mounted on pylons, these fuel tanks were to be mounted from pedestals, with both the tanks and the pedestals being jettisonable.

The first of the futuristic but undeveloped Scorpions were the F-89F and YF-89F. These aircraft were separate Northrop proposals under their project numbers N-81 and N-82, respectively.

These Fs were to be powered by J71-A-3s, as with the actual F-89E. The main differences, however, were in the

wings, which featured a six degree sweepback to their leading edge, and contained leading edge slats. The wing was reduced from 9% to 6% of thickness to chord, a total reduction of 33% over the existing F-89 wing. As with the proposed F-89E, the armament was to be installed in pods located a third of the way out on the wing from the fuselage. Each was to contain forty-two 2.75" FFARs and six Falcon missiles. Also located in the pods were additional fuel cells, and the relocated main landing gear that now consisted of two low-pressure tires. These would retract vertically into the pods, instead of the wing.

A mockup of the N-81 was built, and was inspected by the USAF on May 26, 1952, but as the forecasted weight of the aircraft had increased beyond acceptable limits, the program was terminated three months later.

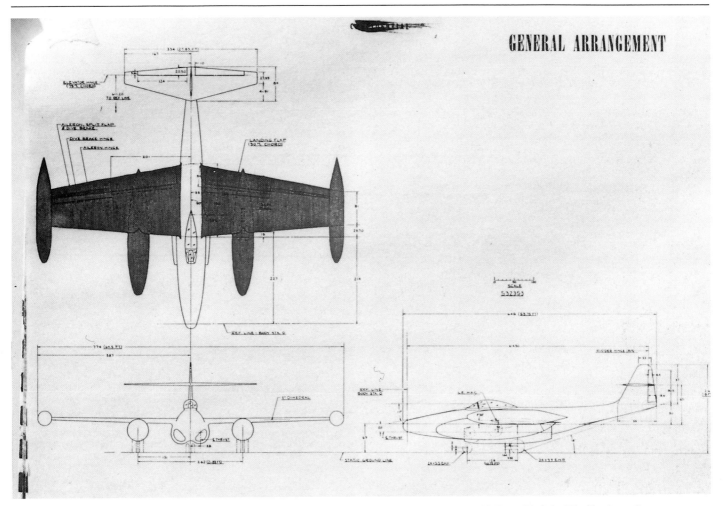

A general arrangement drawing of the proposed F-89F. The wingspan was to be 64' 5", length 53" 7", and height 18'. -Northrop Grumman Corp.

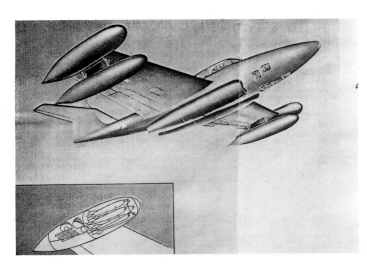

The proposed photo-reconnaissance version of the F-89A featured a camera nose with "pedestal" fuel tanks, which would have given it an estimated range of 1,200 miles. Replacing the wingtip fuel tanks were pods containing airborne radar and camera flash bombs. -Northrop Grumman Corp.

The Delta Scorpion bore little resemblance to the F-89, but it was quite futuristic in comparison. -Northrop Grumman Corp.

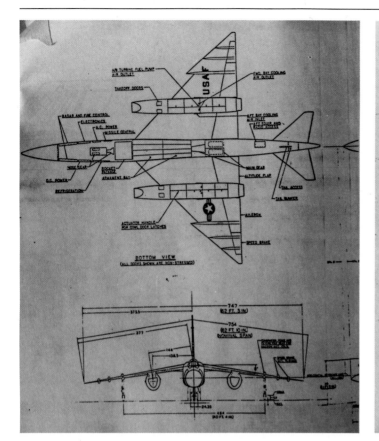

Northrop got into all sorts of esoteric design studies that evolved through a natural progression of their work on the F-89 that took them into the realm of flights of fancy. These included their NS-89, N-144 and N-149 "Delta Scorpions." A general arrangement of the N-149. -Northrop Grumman Corp.

A general arrangement of the NS-89. The N-144 and N-149 were similar in form. They were to be 82' 6" long, span 56' 6" and be 22' 6" in height. -Northrop Grumman Corp

F-89 Survivors & Photo Gallery

Preserved history, 53-2547 was the only interceptor to have live-fired a nuclear armed Genie missile. After finishing its service life with the 186th FIS, the squadron placed it on display at the entrance to their base at Great Falls, Montana. -Kirk Minert

With its paint scheme and markings not quite finished, this ex 179th FIS Scorpion, 53-2677, appears a bit worse for wear at Minneapolis. -Dick Phillips

The pseudo 53-2509 in 449th FIS markings at the Air Force Museum, Dayton, Ohio. The aircraft is actually 52-1911, which had previously served with the 528th ADG, 319th, and 132nd FISs. -MSgt. David Menard, USAF Retired

52-1862 at Tyndall AFB. This Scorpion had served with the 18th FIS in Alaska as a D model, and then with the 84th FIS as a J. It finished its career at James Connelly AFB with the 3565th Pilot Training Wing. -Bill Curry

54-298, a F-89H out to pasture at James Connelly AFB, Texas, Waco, Texas. The base was inactivated in June 1968 and turned over to the Texas State Technical Institute and the F-89 moved to Dyess AFB. -John Kerr

54-231 of the 57th FIS over Iceland in 1958. The 57th FIS was one of the few fighter squadrons assigned directly to MATS, now the Air Mobility Command. -Lt. Col. Steigers

"A the Texan" with a stylized 61st FIS insignia on its nose. The wingtip tanks show evidence of many rocket firings. She was later converted to a J model and served with the 321st FIS. -Saul Kitz via Larry Davis

A lonely appearing flightline at Goose Bay Air Base, and the home of the 59th FIS. 52-2152 had been delivered to the squadron in December 1954 and got a chance to escape to a better climate by participating in the Arizona rocket meet in 1955. -H. Morgan via Menard

One of the early F-89Js with F-89D rocket pods assigned to the 59th FIS. Before conversion it had been assigned to the 18th FIS at Ladd AFB, and later it went to Vermont's 134th FIS. - Arnold Swanberg

Another of the first batch of F-89Js that still featured the F-89D rocket pods. 52-1839 had also served previously with the 18th FIS. Note that the interior side of the rocket pods have also been painted red. -Arnold Swanberg

One of the few F-89Hs assigned to the 176th FIS, circa May 1960, and on display at Olmsted AFB, Pennsylvania. It was a replacement for their D models and the 176th FIS was one of the last ANG squadrons to fly the short-lived H models as they were replaced by J models later in the year. -Frank MacSorley

53-2528 of the 176th FIS on a visit to Byrd Field, Virgina, in January 1962. Wisconsin's ANG squadrons flew more versions of the F-89 than any other: the B, C, D, H, and J. -B. Knowles

53-2649 of the 176th FIS set up for a different role. Note the atmospheric "sniffer" tank on the pylon for upper air sampling. This J example had previously served with the 465th FIS. -B. Knowles

After previously serving with the 66th FIS in Alaska, 51-11416 was assigned to the 126th FIS at Milwaukee. The depiction of the engine turbine warning stripe was unusual on a F-89. -Ron Picciani

Assigned to the 171st FIS at Detroit Wayne Major, these F-89Cs bear a similar paint scheme to the 107th FIS, only the 171st used red as their squadron color. -via Doug Barbier

A nice line-up of pristine 124th FIS F-89Js at Des Moines, Iowa. -Isham Collection

The subject of the decals with Revell's 1/48" scale model of the F-89J. "Golf Hotel Zero Six" (its radio callsign) on the Des Moines ANG ramp. -Merle Olmsted

A "million dollar baby," 53-2513 of the 186th FIS. The initial cost of a modified F-89D to J was $1,008,894.00 but this was later reduced by $20,000.00 as the mass conversion of the 350 example reduced the overall costs. -Greg Gerdes

The second F-89H-5 finished its career with the 123rd FIS at Portland, Oregon. When the squadron switched to J models, they placed it on display for a period, and then it went to Hill AFB, Utah, for further display. It is one of the only two known examples of this model Scorpion still in existence. The original total cost of this aircraft was $988,884.00 with a third of this being its armament system, $335,347.00. -Isham Collection

A beautiful flightline of 116th FIS F-89Js at Geiger Field. The first three examples bear the stencils for having live fired inert Genie missiles. - Isham Collection

53-2642 of the Portland based 123rd FIS. It had originally served with the 433rd FIS at Ladd AFB. - Isham Collection

The end of an era as a "Tub" TF-102 taxies in to start the replacement of 116th FIS Scorpions to Delta Daggers in June 1965. The markings indicated that this particular F-89 had fired three Genies during training exercises -Isham Collection

Having served with no less than five ADC squadrons previously, this F-89J of the 132nd FIS attended an airshow at Hanscom AFB in February 1965. By this time the original sometimes flamboyant ANG paint schemes had given way to to non descript ADC grey with red/orange tip tanks in a corrosion control program. -Isham Collection

One of the last operational F-89Js, 52-1891 of the Maine ANG was photographed at Andrews AFB, Maryland, in November 1968. Six months later the Scorpion was phased out of the ANG's inventory. -J. Morris

52-1838 started its career with the 18th FIS at Ladd AFB. After becoming a J model it then went to the 59th FIS at Goose Bay AB, and then to the 134th FIS at Ethan Allan AFB, Vermont. Installed in the grey rudder fin cap is the command radio antenna, an AN/ARC 27, an eighteen channel (plus Guard) UHF radio. -Isham Collection

Vermont's 134th flew F-89Js from their home base of Burlington Municipal Airport. Previously they had been across the fieldt, but when the 37th FIS was inactivated there in 1960 the 134th obtained all of their assets and control of the base. -K. Minert

53-2607 of the Duluth, Minnesota, based 179th FIS. In 1964 the 179th won the Earl Ricks Trophy Race while their parent unit, the 148th FIG was the first ANG unit to win the USAF's Missile Safety Award. -BGen Wayne Gatlin

F-89Js of the 179th FIS. After all the difficulties with the Falcon missiles, the pylons and associated equipment were removed from the aircraft to reduce its weight and drag. This left the J with only two Genie's, but they were deemed sufficient to destroy a formation of enemy bombers. The lead F-89, No. 50, was the squadron commanders. -BGen Wayne Gatlin

One of the prettiest ANG F-89 paint schemes, as applied to the 179th FIS Scorpions. -BGen Wayne Gatlin

52-2161 was a F-89J assigned to the 132nd FIS at Dow AFB, Bangor, Maine. Previously, as a D model, she had belonged to the 59th FIS at Goose bay AB. - Esposito

All good things must come to an end. In November 1966 the 179th FIS switched from F-89Js to F-102As, of which this example has yet to have its squadron markings applied. -BGen Wayne Gatlin

The NEAC Rocket Team headed for Yuma AFB, Arizona, and the 1955 competition. Yuma was renamed Vincent in October 1956, and was transferred to the USMC in January 1959. -Northrop Grumman Corp.

A gaudy 29th FIS F-89H named, appropriately, "Beach Ball" arrives at Vincent AFB to serve as a radar target during practice interception missions. -Col. F. Storz via B. Leavitt

The EF-89A with the Martin Fire Control System and the rotatable 20mm cannon nose turret. It was assigned to the 2750th Test & Evaluations Group, and eventually wound up as a display aircraft at Lackland AFB, Texas, being repainted in many schemes over the years. -Vince Reynolds

F-89D-35 52-1830 had been one of the prototypes for the F-89H series. It was later modified to a F-89J, and it was later transferred to the US Army as a JF-89J for use with the Radioplane RP-76 drones. It is seen here taxiing to the active at Biggs AFB, Texas. -B. Knowles

"Yes, there are rockets in there." The pod under the nose of this F-89D of the 74th FIS housed a camera for scoring the HVAR firing. -Northrop Grumman Corp.

A F-89D-5 assigned to the US Army for Radioplane missile missions. This Scorpion had F-89J wingtip tanks installed and retained the underwing fueltank pylons to carry RP-76 drones. Note the plexiglas windscreen for the radar observer. -B. Knowles

The NEAC Rocket Team headed for Vincent AFB, Arizona. All of these aircraft were furnished by the 59th FIS. -Northrop Grumman Corp.

Several Air Force bases in Florida were involved in various Scorpion armament and development programs. 49-2448 was the last F-89B-5, a reconfigured A model that was actually the first to be constructed as a B. It was assigned to Patrick AFB, Cocoa Beach, Florida, as a EDF-89B (Exempt Drone Director) and used as a controller for the Snark missile. -Northrop Grumman Corp.

Cockpit Photos

The pilot's instrument panel of a 74th FIS F-89D.-Stanley Wycoff

OPPOSITE: The "office" of a F-89C. -MITER Corp.

The pilots instrument panel of the F-89J on display at the Air Force Museum. Northrop made every attempt to standardize their instrument panels, in contrast to other aircraft manufacturers during the period. -Craig Kaston

An over-all view of a Scorpion's cockpit. The windscreen over the radar observers instrument panel was added to the D and later models to protect the RO from windblast in the case of an inadvertent canopy loss or impending ejection. -Craig Kaston

The RO's instrument panel of a F-89J with the radar scope in a stowed position. If the scope was in the down position and the canopy was ejected, it would automatically snap into the stowed position to facilitate the RO's ejection. -Craig Kaston

The RO's F-89J left console with its myriad electrical circuit breakers. On the longeron are the electrical canopy controls and the canopy lock lever. -Craig Kaston

The RO's right console on a F-89J. The grip is the radar antenna hand control while the dog-leg lever is the emergency hydraulic system hand pump. -Craig Kaston

F-89 Air Defense Squadron Assignments

84th FIS Hamilton AFB, California, commencing June 1951 with F-89Bs replacing F-84s. (To F-86F June 1952, F-94 April 1953-Summer 1955.) F-89D Summer 1955, F-89H Spring 1956, F-89J January 1957. (First ADC F-89J squadron.) F-101B March 1959.

83rd FIS Hamilton AFB, California, commencing Fall 1951 with F-89Bs replacing F-84s. To Paine AFB, Washington, June 1952 with F-86Ds.

27th FIS Griffiss AFB, New York, transition to commence June 1952 with F-89Cs to replace F-86As, but aircraft not received. To F-94C September 1952.

176th FIS Truax AFB, Wisconsin, commencing February 1952 with F-89Cs replacing F-51Ds. To F-51H November 1952. F-89B/C September 1954, F-89D. F-89H August 1958. F-89J January 1960. F-102A Spring 1966.

74th FIS Presque Isle AFB, Maine, commencing June 1952 with F-89Cs replacing F-86As. To Thule AB, Greenland, August 1954. F-89D 1955. Inactivated June 1958.

433rd FIS Activated Truax AFB, Wisconsin, November 1, 1952, with ex-176th FIS F-89Cs. To Ladd AFB, Arkansas, July 1954. F-89D 1955. Returned to ADC control at Minot AFB, Montana, but inactivated without personnel or equipment January 8, 1958.

57th FIS Activated Presque Isle AFB, Maine. Commencing Spring 1953 with F-89C. To Keflavik AB, Iceland, October 1954. F-89D August 1954. F-89J. F-102A July 1962. (Last ADC F-89 squadron.)

61st FIS Ernest Harmon AB, Newfoundland, commencing Fall 1953 with F-89Cs replacing F-94s. F-89D January 1955. Returned ADC April 1957, receiving F-102As November 1957.

18th FIS Minneapolis-St. Paul IAP, Minnesota, commencing Spring 1954 with F-89Ds replacing F-86Fs. (First ADC F-89D squadron.)To Ladd AFB, Arkansas, September 1954. F-102A 1957.0

438th FIS Kinross AFB, Michigan commencing Spring 1954 with F-89Ds replacing F-94Bs. F-102A Summer 1957.

497th FIS Portland IAP, Oregon, commencing Spring 1954 with F-89Ds replacing F-94as. Squadron became a F-86D unit on August 18, 1955, under Project Arrow.

64th FIS Elmendorf AFB, Arkansas, commencing Spring 1954 with F-89C replacing F-94Bs. To ADC August 1957 receiving F-102As.

65th FIS Elmendorf AFB, Arkansas, commencing Spring 1954 with F-89C replacing F-94Bs. F-89D November 1954. To ADC November 1957, inactived January 8, 1958, without personnel or equipment.

66th FIS Elmendorf AFB, Arkansas, commencing Summer 1954 with F-89Ds replacing F-94Bs. To ADC November 1957, inactivated January 8, 1958, without personnel or equipment.

337th FIS Activated Minneapolis-St. Paul IAP, Minnesota. Commencing Summer 1954 with F-89Ds as first mission aircraft. Replaced by 432nd FIS under Project Arrow August 18, 1955.

126th FIS Milwaukee, Wisconsin, F-89B/Cs September 1954 replacing F-51Hs. F-89D, F-89J January 1960. KC-97 June 1960.

449th FIS Ladd AFB, Arkansas, commencing November 1954 with F-89Ds replacing F-94A/Bs. F-89J 1957. Inactivated August 25, 1960.

59th FIS Goose Bay AB, Labrador, December 1954 with F-89Ds replacing F-94s. F-89J Spring 1957. F-102 Spring 1960.

172nd FIS Battle Creek, Michigan, commencing early 1955 with F-89Cs replacing F-86Es. B-57A Spring 1958.

107th FIS Detroit Wayne-Major IAP, Michigan, commencing early 1955 with F-89Cs replacing F-86Es. RF-84F Spring 1958.

171st FIS Detroit Wayne-Major IAP, Michigan, commencing early 1955 with F-89Cs replacing F-86s. RF-84F Spring 1958.

11th FIS Duluth Municipal Airport, Minnesota commencing Spring 1955 with F-89Ds replacing F-86Ds. F-102A August 1956.

58th FIS Otis AFB, Massachussets, commencing Spring 1955 with F-89Ds replacing F-94Cs. F-89H 1956. F-89J 1957. To Walker AFB, New Mexico, August 1959. Inactivated December 25, 1960.

63rd FIS Wurtsmith AFB, Michigan, commencing Spring 1955 with F-89Ds replacing F-86Ds. Replaced by 445th FIS @ Wurtsmith under Project Arrow August 18, 1955.

82nd FIS Presque Isle AFB, Maine, commencing Spring 1955 with F-89Ds replacing F-94Bs. Replaced by 76th FIS @ Presque Isle under Project Arrow August 18, 1955.

437th FIS Oxnard AFB, California, commencing March 1956 with F-89Ds replacing F-94Cs. F-89H July 1956. F-89J March 1958. F-101B January 1960.

318th FIS Presque Isle AFB, Maine, commencing Spring 1955 with F-89Ds replacing F-94Bs. Replaced by 75th FIS @ Presque Isle under Project Arrow August 18, 1955.

75th FIS Presque Isle AFB, Maine, August 18, 1955, upon activation under Project Arrow with F-89D. (Replaced 318th FIS). F-89H Spring 1957. Dow AFB, Maine, June 1959. F-101B Summer 1959.

76th FIS Presque Isle AFB, Maine, August 18, 1955, upon activation under Project Arrow with F-89D. (Replaced 82nd FIS). November 1957 to Pine Castle AFB, Florida. F-89H November 1957. F-89J June 1959. Westover AFB, New York, February 1961. F-102A April 1961.

321st FIS Paine AFB, Washington, August 18, 1955, upon activation under Project Arrow with F-89D. (Replaced 83rd FIS). F-89H Summer 1956. F-89J Fall 1957. Inactivated March 1960.

432nd FIS Minneapolis-St. Paul IAP, Minnesota, August 18, 1955, under Project Arrow with F-89D. (Replaced 337th FIS). F-89H Summer 1956. Inactivated January 1958 (Assets to 109th FIS).

445th FIS Wurtsmith AFB, Michigan, August 18, 1955, with F-89D. (Replaced 63rd FIS under Project Arrow.) F-89H March 1956. (First F-89H squadron.) F-89J Fall 1956. F-101B December 1959.

460th FIS Portland IAP, OR August 18, 1955 under Project Arrow with F-89D. (Replaced 437th FIS.) F-102A May 1958.

465th FIS Griffiss AFB, New York, October 8, 1955, with F-89D upon reactivation. F-89H May 1956, F-89J Spring 1957-July 1, 1959. (Swapped designations with 49th FIS @ Hanscom July 1, 1959, and became a F-86L squadron.)

98th FIS Dover AFB, Deleware, Spring 1956 upon activation with F-89D. F-89H Spring 1957, F-89J Summer 1957-1959. F-101B 1959.

186th FIS Great Falls, Montana, commencing late Spring 1956 with F-89Cs replacing F-94s. F-89H April 1958. F-89J March 1960. F-102A July 1966.

190th FIS Gowen Field, Boise, Idaho, commencing late Spring 1956 with F-89Bs replacing F-94Bs. F-86L July 1959.

29th FIS Malmstrom AFB, Montana, May 1957 with F-89Hs replacing F-94Cs. F-89J Spring 1958. F-101B June 1960.

54th FIS Ellsworth AFB, South Dakota, Summer 1957 with F-89Js replacing F-86Ds. Inactivated December 25, 1960.

123rd FIS Portland IAP, Oregon, commencing June 1957 with F-89D replacing F-94Bs. F-89H July 1958. F-89J March 1960. F-102A January 1966.

179th FIS Duluth IAP, Minnesota, commencing June 1957 with F-89Ds replacing F-94Cs. F-89H November 1959. F-102A November 1966.

132nd FIS Bangor IAP, Maine, commencing September 1957 with F-89D replacing F-94As. F-89J January 1960. F-102A July 1969.

319th FIS Bunker Hill AFB, Indiana, Fall 1957 with F-89Js replacing F-94Cs. F-106A February 1960.

109th FIS Minneapolis-St. Paul IAP, Minnesota, January 1958 with F-89Hs replacing F-94Bs. C-97A January 1960.

116th FIS Spokane IAP, Washington, commencing April 1958 with F-89Ds replacing F-94Bs. F-89J July 1960. F-102A Summer 1965.

134th FIS Ethan Allen AFB, Vermont, commencing April 1958 with F-89Ds replacing F-94s. F-89J July 1960. F-102A 1965.

175th FIS Foss Field, Sioux Falls, South Dakota, commencing May 1958 with F-89Ds replacing F-94Cs. F-102A July 1960.

178th FIS Hector Field, Fargo, North Dakota, commencing May 1958 with F-89Ds replacing F-94Cs. F-102A Summer 1966

15th FIS Davis Monthan AFB, Arizona, F-89J Spring 1959 replacing F-86Ls. F-101B April 1960.

103rd FIS Philadelphia IAP, Pennsylvania, May 1959 with F-89H replacing F-94s. F-89J Summer 1961, C-97 May 1962.

124th FIS Des Moines Municipal Airport, Iowa, April 1962 with F-89Js replacing F-86Ls (assets of 126th FIS). F-84F 1969.

Specifics

	XP-89	F-89B/C	F-89D	F-89H	F-89J
Span	52'	56'	60'5"	59'8"	59'8"
Wing Area	606 sq'	606 sq'	606 sq'	606 sq'	606 sq'
Length	50' 5"	53' 5.5"	53'10"	53'10"	53'10"
Height	17'8"	17'6"	17'6"	17'6"	17'6"
Empty Weight	25,864	B-23,654 C-24,570	25,194	-	-
Weight w/standard fuel load	29,000	B-33,000 C-35,000	41,000	46,600	42,590
Maximum Takeoff Weight	43,910	42,827	46,780	47,400	47,719
Service Ceiling	35,500	50,500	49,200	47,000	43,500
Maximum Speed @ Sea Level	603mph	B-642mph C-650mph	630mph	-	-
Initial Rate of Climb, 1 minute	-	B-10,800 C-12,300	8,300	-	-

Engines

XP-89	Allison J35-A-9 @ 4,000 lbs static thrust
F-89B	Allison J35-A-21A or 24B @ 5,100 lbs static thrust. 6,800 with afterburner
F-89C	Allison J35-A-21/-21A/-33/-33A @ 5,600 lbs static thrust. 7,400 with afterburner
F-89D	Allison J35-A-33A/-41/-35 @ 5,440 lbs static thrust. 7,200 with afterburner
F-89H	Allison J35/35A @ 5,400 lbs static thrust. 7,200 with afterburner

F-89 Serial Numbers

Designation		Contractor #	Serial #'s	Quanity
Model N-24	XP-89	2001	46-678	1
Model N-49	YF-89A	2002	46-679	1
Model N-35	F-89A	2003	No #, static test	1
	F-89A	2004-2012	49-2431/49-2438	8
Model N-35 continued				
	F-89B-1	2013/2015	49-2439/49-2441	3
	F-89B-5	2016/2022	49-2442/49-2448	7
	F-89B-10	2023/2035	49-2449/49-2462	13
Model N-67				
	YF-89D	2036	49-2463	1
Model N-35 continued				
	F-89B-15	2037-2051	49-2464/49-2478	14
Model N-35 continued				
	F-89C-1	2052/2055	50-741/50-744	4
	F-89C-5	2056/2062	50-745/50-751	7
Model N-71				
	YF-89E	2063	50-752	1
Model N-35 continued				
	F-89C-5	2064/2070	50-753/50-759	7
	F-89C-10	2071/2085	50-760/50-774	15
	F-89C-15	2086/2100	50-775/50-789	15
	F-89C-20	2101/2115	50-790/50-804	15
	F-89C-25	2116/2130	51-5757/51-5771	15
	F-89C-30	2131/2160	51-5772/51-5801	30
	F-89C-35	2161/2195	51-5802/51-5836	35
	F-89C-40	2196/2215	51-5837/51-5856	20
Model N-68				
	F-89D-1	2216/2222	51-400/51-406	7
	F-89D-5	2223/2242	51-407/51-426	20
	F-89D-10	2243/2262	51-427/51-446	20
	F-89D-15	2263/2282	51-11298/51-11317	20
	F-89D-20	2283/2322	51-11318/51-11357	40
	F-89D-25	2323/2372	51-11358/51-11407	50
	F-89D-30	2373/2408	51-11408/51-11443	36
	F-89D	2409	No #, static test	1
	F-89D-35	4406/4445	52-1829/52-1868	40
	F-89D-40	4446/4487	52-1869/52-1910	42
	F-89D-45	4488/4532	52-1911/52-1961	50
	F-89D-45	4533/4577	52-2127/52-2165	40
	F-89D-50	4578/4592	53-2447/53-2461	15
	F-89D-55	4593/4652	53-2462/53-2521	60
	F-89D-60	4653/4712	53-2522/53-2581	60
	F-89D-65	4713/4772	53-2582/53-2641	60
	F-89D-70	4773/4817	53-2642/53-2686	45
	F-89D-75	4818/4894	54-184/54-260	77
Model N-138				
	F-89H-1	4895/4954	54-261/54-320	60
	F-89H-5	4955/5050	54-321/54-416	96
	F-89H	5051	No #, static test	1
Model N-160				
	F-89J		Modified from F-89D-35/F-89D-70 blocks: 350	

Bibliography & Acknowledgements

Air International, "*Northrop F-89: Scorpion with a Nuclear Sting*." July 1988, August 1988.

Aviation Week, "*Crosswind Ballistic Testing Uses Seismic Beam System*," May 20, 1957.

Austerman, Wayne R. "*The Final Option*," Airpower, May 1987, 10-19, 54-56.

Cloe, John Hale. *Top Cover For America, The Air Force in Alaska 1920-1983*. Missoula: Pictorial Histories Publishing Company, 1984.

Close, Gilbert, Skyways, "*F-89 All-Weather Interceptor*," December 1951.

Comere, Tom, Ed. *The Air Force Blue Book, Volume 1*. Military Publishing Institute, New York, 1959.

Cornett, Lloyd H. Jr. & Johnson, *Mildred W. Handbook of Aerospace Defense Organization 1946-1980*. Peterson AFB: Office of History, Aerospace Defense Center, 1980.

Correll, John T. ed. "*1992 Almanac Issue*," Air Force Magazine, May 1992

Davis, Larry, & Menard, David. *F-89 Scorpion in Action*. Carrollton: Squadron Signal Publications, 1990.

Detriot News, "*Two Die in Jet at Show*," August 31, 1952.

F-89 Swept Wing Fighter, Northrop Aircraft Inc. Sept. 30, 1949.

Flying, Vol. 48, "*Air Defense Command*," No. 5, May 1951.

Flying, Vol. 52, "*The Air Force*," No. 3, March 1953. 42ff.

Goldberg, Alfred, ed. *A History of the United States Air Force 1907-1953*. Trenton: D. Van Nostrad, 1957.

Great Air Disasters, "*Mid-Air Collision: Near SunLand, California January 31, 1957*," Fawcett, Greenwich, CT, 1962. 104ff.

Green, Bill. *The First Line: Air Defense in the Northeast 1952-1960*. Fairview, Wonderhorse Publications, 1994.

Gross, Charles Joseph. *Prelude to the Total Force: The Air National Guard 1943-1969*. Washington: Office of Air Force History, 1985.

Gunnson, Bill. Aeroplane Monthly, "*Fighters of the Fifties: Northrop Scorpion*," May 1975.

Higham, Robin & Siddall, Abigail, ed. *Flying Combat Aircraft of the USAAF-USAF*. Ames: Iowa State University Press, 1975.

Knaack, Marcelle Size. *Encyclopedia of U.S. Aircraft and Missile Systems*, Volume 1. Washington: Office of Air Force History, 1978.

Life, "*Crash and Catastrophe*," September 5, 1952.

McLarren, Robert. Model Airplane News, "*Black Widow Successor*," February 1949.

Maurer, Maurer. *Air Force Combat Units*. Washington: USAF Historical Division, Air University, Department of the Air Force, 1961,

Maurer, Maurer. *Combat Squadrons of the Air Force in WWII*. Washington: USAF Historical Division, Air University, Department of the Air Force, 1969.

Northrop Service News, "*Arctic Suitability Test*," Vol. 11, No. 6, June 1952.

Pape, Garry R. & Balzer, Gerald H. "*Scorpion: The Story of Northrop's F-89 Long-Range Interceptor*," Airpower, Vol. 11, No. 3, May 1981.

Ravenstein, Charles, A. *Air Force Combat Wings 1947-1977*. Washington: Office of Air Force History, 1984.

Robertson, Bruce, ed. *United States Army and Air Force Fighters 1916-1961*. Letchworth: Harleyford Publications, 1961.

ALSO: Extractions from Air Defense Command Histories 1950-1958: Air National Guard Squadron Histories on file at Headquarters ANGB, the Pentagon, Washington, DC; Highlights of Histories, Alaskan Air Command and its Predecessors 1901-1970 by AAC History Officer E. Marie Salley, Command Historian.

Collections and Extractions from Air Defense Command Fighter Interceptor Squadrons, Air National Guard Fighter Interceptor Squadrons, Alaskan Air Command Fighter Interceptor Squadrons and Northeast Air Defense Fighter Interceptor Squadrons individual unit histories.

Individual Aircraft Record Cards for the F-89 series aircraft.

Acknowledgement goes to the following individuals who provided photographs and support during the writing of this book. Particular acknowledgement goes to John Amrhein and Tony Chong of Northrop Grumman Corporation and David W. Menard for their superlative assistance.

Doug Barbier, Ed Bennett, Roger Besecker, John Cloe AAC Historian, Job Conger/AirChive, William Crowell, Dan Darko, John deVries, Bob Esposito, Mike Fox, Bill Green, Gordon Greer, Cheryl Gumm Edwards Air Force Base History Office, Tom Hildreth, Gordon Homme, Carl Jordan, Craig Kaston, Thomas Kendrick, Bert Kinzey, Roger Lincoln, Barry Miller, Kirk Minert, Ed Morse, Blake Morrison, Douglas Olson, George Partridge, Lionel Paul, Donald Reed, Daniel Riley, Edward Schircely, William Sellars, Bob Stone, Forrest Storz, John Swancara, Oscar Teel.

Requiem for a Scorpion

You can talk of 102s, when you're sipping on the booze,
And the ORI is over, and you've made it.
Then you look out on the line, and you see the '89,
And with all the Tiger in you, man, you hate it!
She's a leaky sneaky Nelly, with a dripping, drooping belly,
And a nasty way of getting aft C. G.
Sure, her silhouette's not neat, and she's got that extra seat,
But she's been pretty good to you and me.

So here's to you, Eighty-Nine, with your long, upswept behind,
Oh, you've caused my mouth to foam,
*When your S. S. A. does roam,
But you've always brought me home,
You Eighty-Nine.

In Arizona's sunny clime, where I used to spend my time,
A'servin' of The Man, in training corps,
Of all that red-hot crew, the finest bird I flew
Was that good ol' grinnnin' gruntin' Eight-Four.
She would sweep you from the dirt, and the G's she'd pull would hurt,
You could turn he inside out, she'd ask for more,
But it really gives you fits when that single engine quits,
Then its silk for you, and sand for Eight-Four.

So here's to you, Eighty-Nine, where the R. O. sits behind,
And those TWO big engines grumble, belch, and whine,
Oh you'll siphon on the roll, as I'm pouring on the coal,
But you'll lift me off the runway every time.

I shan't forget the night, when I dropped behind the flight,
With a cold stone where my belly should have been.
The old girl was sounding queer, I was choaking up with fear,
As that left-hand engine raised a frightful din.

I was dropping out of sight, to the bowels of the night,
And the scream I screamed would raise the roofs of Hell.
But I turned the crossfeed on and the rumble soon was gone,
And she took me home and landed like a pal.

So here's to you, Eighty-Nine,
You grim, ungainly, ugly Eighty-Nine.
When the courage I could beg has gone down to hit the peg,
You'll take me home and land me, like a pal.

Now they talk of 102s, and that's the bird I choose,
I'll fly that Delta Dagger any time,
But I know I'll keep a part of my bleating, beating heart
For that big and brassy, sassy Eighty-Nine.

And we'll meet her later on in the boneyard where she's gone,
Where it's always sand and wind, and no IRAN.

She'll be squatting on the coals, giving flight to damned poor souls,
And we'll get a hop to Hell with Eighty-Nine.

So here's to you, Eighty-Nine,
You solid iron sled, you Eighty-Nine.
Though I've cursed you, and harangued you,
On your landing gear I've pranged you.
You're a better jock than I am,
Eighty-Nine.

*S. S. A., Sideslip Stability Augmentor

Major Marvin L. Randell, 175th FIS: Interceptor Magazine October 1967. Contributed by the Air Force Museum.

Also from the publisher

LOCKHEED F-94 Starfire
A Photo Chronicle

David R. McLaren & Marty Isham

The first U.S. night/all-weather fighter aircraft is chronicled, as is its use by Air Defense Command, Continental Air Command, and Alaska and North-East Air Command, and the Air National Guard.
Size: 8 1/2" x 11" over 220 b/w and color photographs
128 pages   soft cover
ISBN: 0-88740-451-0 $19.95

ROCKWELL B-1B
SAC's LAST BOMBER

Don Logan

This new book covers the complete history of the B-1 Lancer from its inception, through production, and operations with Strategic Air Command.
Size: 8 1/2" x 11" over 400 color & b/w photographs, line drawings, index
256 pages, hard cover
ISBN: 0-88740-666-1 $49.95

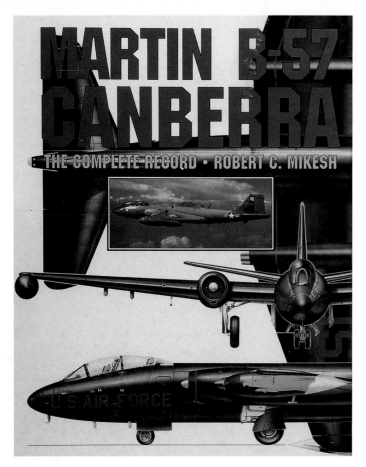

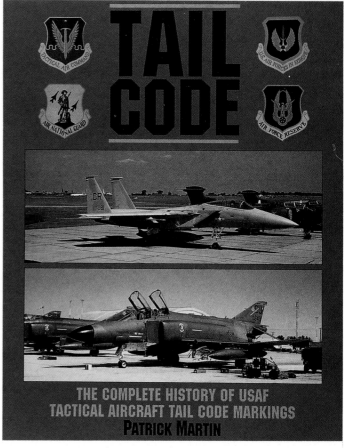

MARTIN B-57 Canberra
The Complete Record

Robert C. Mikesh

A brief history of its British inception sets the stage for the conversion to American standards for production in the United States. The Canberra was needed to fill the night intruder role in the USAF that was identified during Korea and later Vietnam.
Size: 8 1/2" x 11" over 420 color & b/w photographs
208 pages, hard cover
ISBN: 0-88740-661-0 $45.00

TAIL CODE
The Complete History of USAF
Tactical Aircraft Tail Code Markings

Patrick Martin

Full color history covers PACAF, TAC, AFRES, ANG, AAC, USAFE codes and markings.
Size: 8 1/2" x 11"   240 pages   hard cover, over 300 color photos
ISBN: 0-88740-513-4 $45.00